IT GAVE ME
YOU

Praise for
It Gave Me You

"A poignant story about two young people who chose love as their only lifeline, finding joy and quietude in the midst of chaos and pain. This book is born not from the depths of the author's grief, but the scale of her faith: a faith in life, God, humanity, and, ultimately, in the enduring strength of her beautiful and tenacious firstborn daughter. Written with sensitivity and warmth, each page reads like a prayer, feeling an overwhelming sense of gratitude for those fleeting, fragile joys we experience as human beings."

—Lucia Y.

"*It Gave Me You* is a book about connection, hardship, love, and miracles. It does not spare the reader from unimaginable darkness, but instead depicts true love blooming throughout real life trials. In this life, love is faithful, persistent, and undoubtedly divine. Grab your tissues and get ready to witness an eternal love story that will teach you to cherish every moment. This book is a beautiful testimony to God's love and the possibility that God may use your darkest trials to grant you your greatest gifts. For the case of Lexi and Ricky, this was the gift of an undeniable connection and an all-encompassing love that will undoubtedly endure for all eternity."

—Cass S.

"Proof that love and joy can shine in the darkest of environments. A book packed full of love; both romantic and familial."

—Rebecca S., Scotland

"Emily Gould's raw and sincere retelling of her daughter's incredible love story will renew your faith in love. Through all the tragedy of their young lives, Alexis & Ricky will show you that faith & true love will always overcome & endure no matter the circumstance."

—Patty G.

"*It Gave Me You* shares all the parts of the story, not just the glossy social media parts. Life is too short to not be authentic and vulnerable. Lexi lived her life showing us what really matters . . . love!"

—Jamie H.

IT GAVE ME
YOU

EMILY M. GOULD

CFI
An imprint of Cedar Fort, Inc.
Springville, Utah

ISBN 13: 978-1-4621-4573-7

Published by CFI, an imprint of Cedar Fort, Inc.
2373 W. 700 S. Suite 100, Springville, UT 84663
Distributed by Cedar Fort, Inc., www.cedarfort.com

 Library of Congress Control Number: 2023938421

Cover design by Shawnda Craig
Cover design © 2023 Cedar Fort, Inc.
Edited and typeset by Valene Wood

Printed in the United States of America

10 9 8 7 6 5 4 3 2 1

Printed on acid-free paper

This book is written with permission and insight from
Ricky and Alexis Stafford.

To Ash, who lived the ugliest of life and still radiated incomprehensible beauty. To Nana, who taught us to embrace the life we've been given. To Tanner, who brought sunshine into our stormy lives. To Kim, who taught us to live each day to the fullest. To Ali, who sprinkled laughter despite the pain she endured. To Annika, our Warrior Princess, who showed incredible strength against insurmountable odds. And to our beautiful Lex, who encompassed each of us in the safety of her love and constantly radiated light, even on her darkest days.

Learn their stories. Live their legacies. Love them as we do.
#AshtynsArmy
#YnotMe
#ToughlikeTanner
#Kimcankickit
#IwanttobelikeAli
#AnnikasArmy
#AlexisStrong
#StillHere
#StillStrong

Prologue

I BELIEVE IN A LOT OF THINGS. I'M NOT SURE IF LOVE AT FIRST SIGHT is one of those things. Before you chalk me up as a pessimist, allow me to explain. Deep down we all secretly hope for that moment when we see someone for the first time and our eyes meet theirs and everyone else just disappears. The birds sing, the unicorns gallop through puddles of glitter, and life is forever sunshine and rainbows because you have fallen in love in a matter of 0.7 seconds. I don't know if I believe that kind of thing ever really, truly happens to anyone.

However, I do believe in connection at first sight. I believe that two people can meet and be drawn to one another, their souls needing each other far more than their heads or even their hearts may realize at the time. I believe that a connection like that is precious and rare. It must be protected and nurtured. It is powerful yet fragile. It requires hard work and sacrifice.

I'm still undecided about the unicorns and glitter, however, I do know that real, lasting love still exists. Yet, just like all good things in life, it requires hard work and sacrifice. Challenges and trials are as much a part of the tapestry as laughter and lightheartedness. Throw in a few strands of timing, a dose of attraction, and a healthy amount of courage and you're on your way to creating a masterpiece that will be cherished for years to come.

Genuine love usually happens when you least expect it. But love isn't the only thing that happens without warning.

Chapter 1

"Friendship at first sight, like love at first sight, is said to be the only truth." —Herman Melville

"You think I'll need another transfusion today, Mom?" Lexi said as they exited the hospital elevator onto the fourth floor. Her valiant, yet weak, attempt at their top-secret elevator dance party had left Lexi's still recovering body teetering on lethargic.

"Let's hope if you do, that it's only platelets and not another blood transfusion," her mom, Emily, responded. "It's really nice outside today. That's not always common for March in Utah and I don't want you to have to be stuck inside and miss out on the sunshine. The blood transfusions take forever."

"True," Lexi said as she subconsciously placed her hand in the crook of Emily's waiting elbow. Lexi leaned heavily on Emily for support as they fell into a slow rhythm.

"But, I always have more energy after getting blood."

"It's because you're secretly a vampire," Emily said matter-of-factly. Their steps shuffled down the hospital corridor as people walking at a normal pace buzzed past them.

"What gave it away?" Lexi said as she humored Emily's pitiful attempt at humor.

"The fangs," Emily replied. "But don't worry, we love and accept you for who you are."

Lexi let out a small chuckle and they slowly continued their walk arm in arm towards the oncology clinic. Lexi's 5'7" frame hunched over slightly from the unrelenting pain and her bones seemed to grind against each other with every step. Gone were the days of her long, lean dancer's body. It had abandoned her almost as quickly as her long, dark hair. Her eyes were still blue, but they now appeared in more sunken sockets and were framed with dark circles rather than dark lashes. Her skin was no longer tan and sun kissed with freckles but pale and marred with the scars of her ongoing battle.

To the naked eye, Lexi's physical appearance would now place her among the frail, the bruised, and the broken. But her mind would never let go of the mental strength she possessed. It was one of the only things this disease couldn't rip from her. It had been a mere six weeks since she had gone in for surgery to remove a malignant tumor in her abdomen, only to go in for an emergency surgery just two days later. She clocked some hard time in the ICU before graduating to the surgical floor for recovery. After several weeks of intense physical therapy, Lexi had finally broken free of the tubes and drains protruding from her body and been allowed to go home. Unfortunately, surgery was only the halfway point in her treatment plan or "road map" as the doctors called it. Blasted cancer.

Lexi and Emily inched their way towards the clinic and Emily used her knee to push the button that activated the automatic door. It was flu season and, given Lexi's history over the past six months, they weren't willing to take any chances with unnecessary germs that could be contracted by using their hands to touch a public button. Who knew when the last time that germ hangout had been sanitized? Emily subconsciously shook her head at the acknowledgement of her compulsiveness, brushing it aside. It was life now. They were all just trying to survive.

Arm in arm, they entered the clinic and began to routinely sanitize their hands. It didn't matter that they had sanitized when they first entered the hospital, and then again when waiting for the elevator. Out of necessity, sanitizing had become their new favorite hobby; something that was second nature to them both these days.

"Hey ladies!" the receptionist said with a kind smile. Her dark hair ended just above her shoulders and her kind eyes beamed brightly behind her stylish tortoise-shell glasses.

"How are we today?"

"We're good, how are you?" Lexi replied back with a smile of her own. She didn't particularly enjoy coming to the hospital but the company made up for it.

"Look at you!" a nearby nurse said. "You aren't even in your wheelchair. Is it parked outside the doors?"

"No," Lexi said with a sense of pride as her worn-out body was led by the medical technician, Paige, to be weighed. "I walked all the way in from the parking lot today. We were going pretty slow, but I did it."

"That's amazing, Lex!" Paige said with genuine love and admiration. She paused and allowed Lexi a moment to catch her breath. Lexi mentally crossed her fingers and stepped up to be weighed. Her shoulders grew heavy, but not heavy enough to change the number on the scale. Down another pound and a half. She felt deflated. The constant pull to feed a body that clearly no longer wanted food was weighing on her. Not literally, of course, or her skin might not be draped on her skeleton frame without the muscle that used to act as a filler. But emotionally, the toll that her lack of weight took on her was real. It was more than real. It was defeating. Her clothes hung on her like an ill-fitting robe. She had long abandoned leggings and fitted shirts. Instead, she tried to hide behind the cover of sweaters and joggers. But, her body bore witness to the truth every time she looked in the mirror. She was a fraction of the girl she was before, in more ways than she had the energy to count. Paige lovingly patted Lexi's arm, recorded her weight and carefully helped her to a nearby chair so that the intake process could be completed.

The child-sized blood pressure cuff squeezed Lexi's teenage arm as she asked Paige about her nail polish. The conversation went from nail polish to family to treatment as Paige charted Lexi's vitals. With a steady hand from Emily, Lexi stood and appraised her next goal. She just had to make it down the hall to a treatment room. Paige led the way in her brightly printed scrub top and identifying gray scrub bottoms. Her chestnut hair bobbed as she walked and her eyes danced when Lexi asked her how her grandchildren were doing.

Clinic rooms lined the short hallway like soldiers at attention. Today Lexi's post would be the last door on the right. She exhaled and began her march. Lexi looked at the doors as she slowly passed. She had been stationed at each room at least once during the past six months. Her thoughts turned to the young warriors behind those doors today. What battle lay in store for them? Were they being discharged from treatment with the knowledge that they had valiantly completed their task? Were they being asked to step down from the ranks, knowing that although their hearts were willing, their bodies were no longer fit for war? After months or even years on leave were they being called back into active duty? She said a soldier's silent prayer for them as she held Emily's arm just a little tighter. What orders lay behind her closed door today?

The sterile atmosphere of the hospital used to feel arid and bleak to Lexi. The white walls spotted with vomit bag dispensers and sanitizer at random intervals, which she constantly made use of, had served as a perpetual reminder that she was no longer normal. However, in time, the scene went from one of mocking cruelty to one of peaceful serenity. During the past few months Primary Children's Hospital had become somewhat of a second home to Lexi, the staff and occupants a makeshift family. Since being diagnosed with cancer, Lexi felt as if she had spent more time at the hospital than in her own home. Between her inpatient chemo treatments, and the long stays from unexpected illnesses and surgeries, she wasn't far off.

Lexi urged her body forward, keeping her eyes on the door to her clinic room. Her muscles groaned in protest, and she felt as if she were at least eighty years older than her fifteen years. Her mind reeled that only a few short months ago she could dance for hours without tiring. Now, she felt arthritic and brittle after a simple, short walk.

Lexi heard familiar music coming from the room across the hall and it offered a slight distraction from the discomfort that her slow saunter brought. She was clearly too weak to dance, but her inner dancer would not be stopped from bobbing subconsciously to the beat.

"Someone's got some good taste in music," Lexi said aloud to no one in particular.

"That's Ricky," Paige said brightly, motioning with her head to the room that "Hot Line Bling" by Drake was playing from. "You've met him, haven't you?"

Lexi replied "no" with a slight shake of her head, refocusing on her destination. She always enjoyed meeting new cancer friends and seeing the light in their little eyes when they saw that she was bald and had a port just like they did. But, she knew she wouldn't have the strength to crouch down to talk to a new friend right now. She'd need to be seated before meeting anyone today. Perhaps if she could just make it to a chair she'd be able to come close to eye level with whatever small friend she was about to meet. Lexi continued inching towards her room which was a mere three feet away now. She could all but reach out and grab the door handle if she didn't need Emily's arm for support. Her body was beginning to shake slightly from the pain and exertion. She felt Emily brace her carefully and instinctively slow her pace. Lexi gave her a slight nod, a sign in their unspoken language that meant she was okay to keep going.

"I'll be right back, Lex," Paige said. She quickly left to knock on the door of the room that the music was coming from. It happened to be the room just across from Lexi's. Lexi and Emily didn't wait to see who answered but continued the journey into their room and the promise of rest that it offered. Emily barely had a moment to put their things down before Paige reappeared, but she was not alone. Lexi slowly turned and felt her mouth crack open in disbelief.

Out in the hall stood a 6'2" tall, healthy looking young man; a stark contrast to the age and physical attributes of the friends that Lexi usually encountered in the cancer clinic. He was wearing a Nike T-shirt and basketball shorts. His body was not hunched over in pain, and he didn't look to be limited in any area. He was not sad, scared, angry, or even bald. He was just a normal teenager, the kind she used to be.

"Lexi, this is Ricky. Ricky, this is Alexis," Paige said with a wry smile. She then quickly said her goodbyes and returned to her station and duties checking the vitals on the next patient. The childhood cancer clinic was always far too busy than it ever should be.

"Hey!" Ricky said kindly.

"Hi!" Lexi replied with a quick smile. Her need to sit down was somehow curbed by intense curiosity. "My mom and I were just eavesdropping on your music."

"Aw, ya like that?" Ricky replied easily. "I'm a big fan of Drake—well, that and making my momma laugh, and she's always laughing when I'm trying to dance. This is my mom, Maren," Ricky added, motioning just behind him.

A woman with dark brown hair pulled into a braid stepped forward and greeted Lexi and Emily with a warm smile. She was about Lexi's height, if Lexi had been able to stand upright. Emily took a minute to introduce herself. The two women quickly slipped into typical mom conversation.

Lexi used the brief time during the exchange to get a good look at Ricky. If his height and athletic build didn't set him apart, the stuff growing on top of his head surely did. Lexi seemed both confused and intrigued by the fact that this young man was sporting a full head of hair in contrast to the stark nakedness of her scalp. She stared unabashed for a moment as she took in the boy before her. Ricky rotated between adding to the mom-conversation and stealing sidelong glances at the bald girl he had just met.

Lexi's legs thrummed from the physical exertion she'd put them through in the last twenty minutes, but she no longer felt a desire to retreat to the chair in her room. Her curiosity got the better of her as her bluntness won out.

"What type of cancer do you have?" she blurted out, wondering about his motives for spending time in a cancer clinic when he was clearly very healthy. Surely, there were so many other places this guy could be.

"I had leukemia but I'm in remission now," Ricky said with a triumphant grin. It was clear that smiling was something that came natural to him. "I'm just finishing up treatment."

Lexi returned his smile with a genuine one of her own and congratulated him on his recent victory.

"Do you have leukemia too?" Ricky asked, conversationally. He had to remind himself not to stare at this girl. It wasn't that she was bald. He had seen plenty of bald kids in his life, he had been the "bald kid." He wasn't quite sure what it was. There was something about her eyes. She only had a few of her lashes left. He wasn't sure if they were still falling out or trying to make a comeback, but it didn't matter. Her eyes were a clear, startling shade of blue. They held a light that set her apart from anyone he had met before. *Blink,* Ricky reminded himself. *She's going to think you are weird if you don't blink.*

"I have this scar right here from my port," Ricky exclaimed, before giving Lexi a chance to respond to his previous question. Before he knew what he was doing, he found himself lifting the bottom hem of his shirt. He revealed a small, one and a half inch mark that was left from the device that was placed in his chest during treatment. The scar was high enough on his chest that it could have easily been shown by pulling down the collar of his shirt as opposed to showcasing his abs. But he didn't care. He had worked hard to get those muscles back after being hit with chemo. If he could put them to use in impressing this girl today, he wasn't about to miss the opportunity.

"Do you have one of these?" he asked with intrigue in his eyes. He already knew the answer. Every cancer kid had one of these scars because every cancer kid he had ever met had a port. He was just searching to find something in common with this girl. Lexi smiled coyly and opted to do some impressing of her own.

"Yeah, I do have one of those scars. I still have my port in," she said as she pulled on the collar of her shirt to reveal the small scar and the lump under her skin from her unaccessed port. "I also have this scar from where they removed my tumor. It's pretty cool, too," she said nonchalantly as she raised the bottom of her shirt to reveal a large scar that began high on the back of her rib cage, wrapped itself towards the middle of her abdomen and curved downwards past her belly button. "I have neuroblastoma—it's cancer of the nerves. My tumor was about the size of a cantaloupe, and it ruptured so they had to cut me open from clear back here," she said as she gestured with her finger. "They cut through my diaphragm and then all the way down my belly." The casualness in her tone made it clear that she'd had to recite this story before.

"Dang!" Ricky said somewhat under his breath as he lowered his shirt. It was clear he would need to find another avenue if he were going to dazzle this girl.

"Two days later they opened me back up and gave me this one," Lexi said as she gestured to the part of her scar that extended a few inches above her belly button. "My insides were on my outsides twice in forty-eight hours. Pretty cool, huh?"

"That's crazy . . ." Ricky said with an air of disbelief that someone seemingly so fragile talked of things so heavy with such a lightness.

"So what school do you go to?" he asked, changing the subject. He knew it was only a matter of time before the doctors came and either he or Lexi would need to leave. The cancer clinic wasn't really the easiest place to get to know a girl, he decided.

"I'm a sophomore at Cyprus High," Lexi replied, then added quickly, "It's in Magna—just west of here."

"I know where Cyprus is," Ricky said with another smile. Lexi found herself enjoying the ease with which this boy created conversation, and equally affected at the genuine ease of his smile. Most guys her age tended to be lacking in their communication skills. It was as if they had no emotion or too much emotion when talking to a girl. In her limited experience, it seemed as if the opposite sex was either ready to commit for life or believed that they couldn't say hi to a girl without her falling hopelessly in love with them. Even before cancer, Lexi didn't see the point in riding the roller coaster of teenage emotions. Now, she knew the attraction would just make her sick.

This conversation with Ricky felt different—there was no pressure, no expectations. Although she'd just met Ricky, they talked easily and comfortably, like old friends who were becoming acquainted once again. Ricky didn't seem bothered or impressed by her lack of hair. His eyes didn't randomly glance at her bald head just to see if her hair had magically reappeared. There was no pity in his tone. He just treated her the way everyone used to treat her—like a regular teenage girl.

"We played you guys in basketball last year," Ricky said.

"You play basketball?" Lexi asked.

"Yeah, I love it. That's one of the reasons I'm excited to finish up the oral chemo they have me on—I'm ready to start getting stronger and start playing the way I used to be able to play. Do you play any sports?" asked Ricky. He found himself becoming more relaxed around this girl. Her very presence encouraged an undeniable peace.

"This is my second year on the drill team," Lexi replied and then wistfully added, "but I haven't been able to compete or anything since I was diagnosed. I'm usually in the hospital when the competitions are anyway." Lexi's heart flashed briefly to a life before cancer. Her countenance reacted ever so subtly to the change. She quickly recovered with a slight smile, but not before Ricky saw the effort behind it.

Ricky's mind reverted back to a sterile hospital room—his body was weak, his face swollen from the medicine he was on. He didn't recognize himself in the small mirror that hung above the sink just three feet from his bed. A team of doctors entered his room and Ricky greeted them warmly. Ricky asked about his upcoming treatment, wondering how much more he would have to endure before returning to his team, his friends, his life. The lead doctor smiled but the action did not reach his warm green-brown eyes.

"Ricky, like I've told you before" the doctor began with practiced patience, "even when you are done with treatment, your body won't be able to go back to doing the things it was able to do before. We are working to get you cancer free and we need you to do your part, but that also comes at a price. The chemo that you are taking has lasting effects. It is very likely you will never play competitive basketball again. If by some miracle you are able to maybe play on a high school team, you will never be able to play at the same level you did before being diagnosed." Ricky's face fell. He couldn't control it. It just fell. The hope. The happy. The future. It just fell right out of him. Who was he if he couldn't play basketball? His shoulders slumped as the strings of what would be had been cut unexpectedly.

Ricky shook the memory and the accompanying emotion from his psyche. The feeling of not being well enough to do what you wanted most to do still haunted him. He saw the same desire in Lexi's eyes. A look of hunger that would never be satiated, thirst that would never be satisfied. He understood too well the struggle of trying to make your body be healthier than it actually was, and the ultimate heartache at the realization that there were some circumstances in life that no amount of willpower could change.

"You're still a part of the team, Lexi," Ricky said bluntly, a fierceness in his eyes confirming the power in his sentence. The weight of his words spoke to Lexi's soul. He wasn't trying to placate her concerns or pacify her worries as a father would a small child. He meant what he said with such genuineness that it took her aback. His words gave her a sense of belonging in an isolated world.

"Plus, if you said this is your second year, that means that you made the team as a freshman. You must be really good."

Lexi shrugged her shoulders with a grin and said, "I've been dancing since I was three and I really love it. I can't wait to get back to doing it again." A fierceness that belied the calming spirit that surrounded her burned deeply in her crystal blue eyes. It threw Ricky off his game momentarily and he worked quickly to recover. There was no doubt this girl could accomplish anything she put her mind to.

"So, if you're a sophomore does that mean that you are sixteen?" Ricky asked, trying to gauge Lexi's age.

"I'm actually fifteen," she replied. "I'm really young for my grade. I turned 15 and was diagnosed exactly one month later."

"Hey!" said Ricky "We're the same! I was diagnosed when I was fifteen too. I'm seventeen now, though. I'm a junior."

Lexi didn't have the chance to respond before her team of doctors came and broke up the hallway conversation. Before Ricky knew it, she had said goodbye and the door to her room closed. Ricky wondered what type of news that closed door would hold for his new friend today. He prayed it would be good.

As the heavy door and the conversation with Ricky solidly closed, the discussion on Lexi's next step in treatment began. Although she liked her doctors, Lexi never enjoyed these conversations. It was behind these closed doors that all of the lasting effects of the cancer war games were spoken aloud. The truth behind shining bald heads and smiling round faces was pulled from the dark crevices that social media kept buried. The intimate details of a life sentence that seemed too heavy for even the guiltiest of souls was placed upon innocent hearts. Lexi listened as long as she could to what her body would go through; the long-term problems she'd battle every day just to live a "normal" life. At the end of the conversation it was always the same thing, "Do you have any questions, Lex?" She did, but none that she dared voice. Not that it would matter if she did. No one seemed to have any concrete answers when it came to her disease.

Lexi had learned early on that cancer was tricky in more ways than one. It wasn't like getting strep. It wasn't as simple as a throat swab followed by medication and a time frame of when you should start feeling better. Cancer was like a black hole that doctors did their best to understand but could never fully explain. Cancer did what it wanted, when it wanted, and teams of geniuses everywhere did their best to outsmart it. Lex was grateful for the brilliant people that had already worked so hard to save her life; certain that she wouldn't still be alive without them. But she had to force her body into doing its part if she stood any chance of living past her teen years.

The thin hospital tissue paper crinkled under Lexi as it tore with every movement she made. The sound used to bother her, but now it was just part of the hospital soundtrack. Each sound worked in harmony with those around it. The beeping monitors, the hum of the pumps as they delivered fluid to the patients, the push of the automatic doors, and the squish of sanitizer all played a role in a makeshift ensemble. The symphonies that featured children's laughter were her favorite; the ones that featured their cries caused her heart physical angst.

The doctors reviewed Lexi's labs, her blood work, and how her body had been recovering from her last infusion of chemo. The sheer memory of the six rounds of chemo she'd endured made her physically ill. She had been sick before, but she couldn't adequately describe what that poison had done to her. She wondered if she would ever again be the same. Her shoulders gave an involuntary shiver, and she swallowed the bile that instinctively rose in her throat.

Tandem autologous transplants were the next stop on Lexi's road map. Apparently, one transplant wasn't enough for her cancer, so the doctors were telling her she would need two. She let her legs swing casually and the crinkling tissue paper responded in kind. Lexi adjusted slightly on the examination table and felt it tear. She repositioned and the paper ripped again, this time under the pressure of her hand. She wasn't particularly taken with hospital protective paper in general, but today it held a certain allure. That allure came in the form of distraction from reality. The longer she could busy herself with the slight creases, slits, and tears, the more likely she was to be spared the details of the upcoming transplants. She didn't need to listen to this soundtrack. She would live the nightmare soon enough.

Lexi allowed her mind to rejoin the conversation just in time to hear that she would get to spend two weeks (with the exception of clinic visits and as needed transfusions) at home with her family before coming back to the hospital for her first transplant. *Two weeks!* The thought of two straight weeks at home made her smile. If she wasn't saving her energy for the walk to the car, she might have even done a little dance. She focused on the promise of family movie nights and the thought of sibling sleepovers as she let her mind wander to the countless possibilities that two whole weeks with her family could hold as the rest of the side effects were listed. She'd have to listen to them again at the next appointment anyway.

Lexi and Emily thanked the doctors as they finished up and said their goodbyes. Emily began packing up their belongings in preparation to head to the back of the clinic. Arm in arm, they slowly shuffled back down the hall and towards their new station. Emily helped Lexi lower herself into the recliner and walked a few feet to the community refrigerator to grab a few snacks on the off-chance Lexi would be hungry.

"Maren just friended me on Facebook," Lexi told Emily.

"Cool!" Emily said in response as she held up a Sprite, a small package of goldfish crackers, and a standard issue vomit bag. Lexi thanked her for remembering to grab all of the supplies that snack time included. Just then Emily's phone buzzed. "Hey, me too. She just sent me a message," Emily said, as she took a seat in the chair next to Lexi's recliner. A nurse began accessing Lexi's port and flushing her central line in preparation for her platelet transfusion. Lexi crinkled her nose involuntarily as the saline was pushed from the syringe through her port and into her veins. The salty taste made its way from her veins into her taste buds.

"She said that it was good meeting us, that they hope things go well with your treatment, and they hope to see us again soon," Emily added.

"That's really nice of her," Lexi said. "I wouldn't mind seeing them again. Ricky was really funny and it was nice being able to have someone my age to talk to that understands some of what I'm going through. He's all done with his treatment though. So, I'm not sure if I'll actually see him again." She paused for just a moment before adding, "But, I hope so."

Chapter 2

"A friend is one that knows you where you are, understands where you've been"—William Shakespeare

Ricky's appointment could not have gone better. All of his labs were completely normal and the doctors still considered him NED or "no evidence of disease." He breathed a sigh of relief at hearing those words, although these days he was becoming less and less fearful of relapse. Cancer was in the past and he was focused on his future. He could feel his body rebuilding itself slowly after the decimation cancer had caused. Each day his bones became stronger and his strength more defined. His hair had some back with a slight curl at first, not that he minded at all. The curls coupled with the fact that he had survived cancer seemed to get him a little more attention from his female classmates, something he would never be upset about. But, cancer was a crummy café on the road trip of his life. He wouldn't want to stop there again, but he was grateful to say he had experienced it once.

Sure, it had been a pit stop laced with toxins, poisons, and all sorts of other deadly things, but it wasn't all bad. Overall, Ricky felt as if he had been able to navigate his way through his cancer journey fairly unscathed. The lasting effects of his treatment hadn't limited his ability to play basketball, he just had to work harder in order to get back what had come naturally to him before. But, it wasn't just making it through cancer that had given Ricky gratitude for the experience. Cancer had changed him. It was more than just the physical process of losing his hair and his strength, or even the mental aspect of missing out on everyday life that had reshaped him. Ricky's metamorphosis occurred over time. Like the drops of chemo that had dripped from the IV bag methodically into the tubing and eventually found their way into his veins. Ricky's transformation took place as he walked in the halls of his high school. Once confident in his appearance, he watched helplessly as his face took on the resemblance of a chipmunk storing nuts for the winter. It happened as he was mocked for his bald head during a basketball game by some, cheered on for his courage to play by others. His evolution came at the realization that he wanted nothing more than to just play the game he loved without the caveat that now existed every time he picked up a basketball. It had been a process to get from who he was before cancer to the young man he was today. As he reminisced deeper, Ricky recalled a singular event that still sent a calming warmth to each of his extremities.

When Ricky was first diagnosed, he was terrified of losing his hair. The memory of the emotion caused a melancholy smile to tug at the corner of his mouth. How naive he had been. Hair loss paled in comparison to what he went through, and what he went through paled in comparison to what others endured. Still, the thought of being the bald kid with no eyebrows felt like social suicide. He spent hours begging and pleading with Heavenly Father to please spare his hair from the inevitable effect of chemo. He could handle being the cancer kid. He wasn't sure if he could stomach looking like the cancer kid. Five months into treatment and his prayers were still being answered. In contrast to the shining heads of the other kids he met in the clinic, Ricky's dark locks let him cling to the illusion that perhaps he wasn't quite as sick as the doctors said he was.

Then, one day all of that changed. The shift in attitude that Ricky had towards his cancer hit him as abruptly as a basketball to the back of his hair-covered head. He'd walked into his kitchen just in time to see Maren hang up her cell phone. The back door slammed shut as a pair of his younger brothers, clothed for summer in cut-off shorts and bare chests, ran outdoors for yet another sunshine adventure. He watched them go and wondered for only a moment what hidden treasures the day might hold for them. However, the drawn look on Maren's face stifled his curiosity completely as he turned his full attention to her.

Sensing Ricky's eyes on her, Maren began. "That was the doctor." She looked as if the words were rotting in her mouth, but she didn't know how to spit them out.

"Okay," Ricky said. "What did he say?"

"Ricky, your chemo isn't working."

A chill ran up Ricky's spine. What did she mean it wasn't working? Why would they give him chemo if it wasn't working? Chemo killed cancer cells, that's what it did. It couldn't just "not work." When he didn't respond, she looked at him frankly. Her brown eyes usually held flecks of amber like little bits of adventure were trapped inside just waiting to break free, but as she held his gaze now he saw only the matte brown of her irises gazing back at him.

"Ricky, have you been praying about your cancer?" Maren asked directly.

"Yes," Ricky said without hesitation. He knew his prayers were being heard as well; the answer made manifest in the fact that he was still needing haircuts.

"What, *exactly*, are you praying for?" Maren asked pointedly. Her tone was neither conversational nor accusatory. If Ricky had to assign it an emotion he would call it a three-way tie between frustration, desperation, and helplessness. She stared at him as she waited for an answer.

"I've been praying that I would keep my hair through treatment," he said simply, realizing by the look in her eyes that this answer might not be the one she was looking for. He quickly added, "I really don't want to be bald." Justifying his reasoning felt needed.

Frustration and desperation were now battling for first place on Maren's face. Helplessness was no longer in the running.

"You know that you have the Philadelphia chromosome, right?" Maren said, worry creeping through the frustration in her question.

"Yeah," Ricky said, not wanting to be reminded of his disease or anything related to it.

"That chromosome is only present in about 5% of patients. But when it is, it automatically classifies you as high risk. You only have a 20–30% chance of beating cancer with chemo alone. If you want to survive, and do so without a bone marrow transplant, I suggest taking some time to think about the things you're praying for. It's time to decide what really matters."

Ricky's conversations with God changed that night. He prayed with hope. He pleaded with fervor. He petitioned with faith. But his actions were no longer motivated by his physical appearance. His focus had changed from what he wanted, to what God needed from him. That night he prayed that the chemo would begin to work. No caveats. No conditions. His focus had changed from what he wanted to what God needed from him. Ricky pled with God to save his life. He did not want to die. The following morning his pillow was covered with several large clumps of his dark brown hair. Within two days he was completely bald.

A slight prickle ran up Ricky's spine as he shook the memory from his thoughts. He ran his fingers subconsciously through his thick, dark hair. There was something about losing everything he once valued that helped Ricky gain the greatest gift he had been given— the unyielding knowledge that God not only lived, but that He loved him and was aware of him. Hard as he tried, the words of his mouth never seemed to do justice to the feelings of his heart when it came to expressing the depths of what he had gone through. However, those experiences were now only memories. He could say with a surety that he had gone through something hard and was now ready to live out the rest of his days in utter bliss.

Ricky plopped down easily on the couch in his living room. Danja, Ricky's ister, and his brothers were still at school. Maren had retreated to the garage to pick up where she had left off on her latest project. He pulled out his phone and opened Instagram. He tapped the search bar and typed in the name "Alexis Gould." Immediately his query returned the desired results as images of the girl he'd met earlier that day filled his screen.

There were multiple images of Lexi laughing with her siblings or hugging them tightly. It looked like she was the oldest in her family, just like Ricky was. There were a few selfies with positive quotes as the caption, and pictures of different trips she had gone on or adventures she had experienced. Then there were the drill team pictures. Ricky knew dancing was Lexi's passion simply by the way that she spoke of it, but the pictures of her in her performance makeup weren't his favorite. The makeup was meant to make her look like everyone else on her team. Of course this wasn't possible. Even after one interaction he knew he would be able to pick Lexi out of a crowd. A girl like that wasn't meant to blend in.

Then came the first picture of Lexi with no hair. A bald fifteen-year-old girl with startling blue eyes and a sprinkling of freckles across the bridge of a petite nose. Lexi was closest to the camera and Emily was smiling right behind her. The caption read, "Today was hard but I'm so thankful I have her to make me smile. <3".

Ricky remembered the feeling of going bald at fifteen and the emotions that came with it, but Lexi seemed to be somewhat unscathed by her lack of hair. Her smile was just as beautiful, and her eyes filled with possibly more light than before she'd lost her hair. Given the option, he was sure that she would prefer to have her locks back, but looking through her Instagram account, her hair did not seem to dictate who she was. She did not try to hide her bald head; on the contrary, it was visible in almost every recent picture she took. No hats, scarves, or wigs. Just a perfectly round head that shone when the lighting was right. Ricky was fascinated that a girl could be just as beautiful with hair as she was without, but somehow Lexi was. Her blue eyes sparkled and the tiny freckles across her almost too small nose complimented her skin tone perfectly. Her lack of hair highlighted her other physical features in the same way that the loss of one of the five senses causes the remaining senses to heighten their performance.

Ricky scrolled through the photos a second time. He looked closer at them, trying to figure out what it was about this girl that had him so captivated. He had seen pretty girls before, beautiful ones even. But there was something about Lexi. She didn't seem to be aware of her beauty or the effect it had on those around her. Oddly enough, that only mesmerized him more. In his experience, teenage girls often enjoyed the spotlight and the attention that accompanied it. However, something told him that wasn't the case with Lexi

Okay, Ricky thought to himself as he exhaled. *So, how am I going to talk to her?* What would he say to a girl like that? It was clear she wouldn't be impressed with the normal things that seemed to impress girls his age. She was going through cancer herself, so he couldn't play the *I'm a rock star because I just beat cancer* card. She excelled in dance, so she likely wouldn't be impressed by his amazing athletic ability. For the first time in a long time, Ricky Stafford felt completely off his game.

Ricky had always done his best to hold his standards high. He worked hard, he played hard, he prayed hard. Thanks to his bout with cancer, he was well known in his community. That knowledge coupled with his basketball abilities and a bit of teenage testosterone produced the perfect mix for a very confident young man. He knew he was likable and had never had a problem making friends. His charismatic nature ensured that he was never without an admirer, and his natural charm ensured that he didn't have to exude much effort to capture a heart. In fact, he had become somewhat accustomed to catching the attention of young women with minimal, if any, effort. So, trying to talk to Lexi shouldn't be that hard. But for some reason it was. Lexi was different from any other girl, and he knew it. He couldn't just follow her on Instagram and send her a message, hoping she would respond. He wondered how many guys had tried the same thing and how many unopened messages she had. He closed Instagram determined to not be just another unread message. He needed to come up with a better plan.

Two weeks passed far too quickly and before Lexi knew it, she found herself walking through the double doors of the hospital for her first stem cell transplant. Emily laughed easily as Lexi expounded every bit of her energy in order to keep the tradition of their elevator dance party alive. Her attempt was weak at best, but they both loved the ritual anyway.

The elevator opened with a ding onto the fourth floor. Lexi and Emily stepped out of their silver surroundings and into their comfort zone as they headed to the cancer unit and the friendly faces that awaited them there. They began to settle into what would be their home for the next month. Emily unpacked their items as nurses came in and out of the room to take Lexi's vitals and chart her ever-declining weight. They chatted friendlily about the upcoming transplant as easily as old friends converse about the weather. Lexi's team of doctors had simplified what was to be expected over the coming weeks.

In layman's terms, a few months ago they had drawn a bunch of Lexi's blood (before the chemo destroyed it) and had taken out the cells that were responsible for making all of the other cells. The process was known as stem cell harvesting. The days ahead would consist of fatal doses of chemo being administered for a full week in hopes of killing all of the cells in Lexi's body. Unfortunately, chemotherapy cannot distinguish between healthy cells and cancer cells so everything had to be hit. Everything would be sacrificed so that the cancer didn't come back. After that, the healthy cells from the harvesting would be re-administered back into Lexi's system. The hope was that these healthy cells would start doing their job so that her body would start working again and remain cancer free. The whole process was supposed to take about a month. When she was stable enough to go home, she'd be discharged for a few weeks before doing it all again. It wasn't exactly how she had planned on spending her summer, but there were worse things.

The doctors had told Lexi to plan for a month-long stay for each transplant. But, by the amount of luggage Emily brought in, one would think they were preparing to be inpatient for at least the next decade. Lexi watched in amusement as Emily unpacked the clothes first, followed by the toiletries. The gel pens and art supplies were followed by the gel nail light and at least twenty-five different colors of polish. Emily had just set the laptop down and went to work making her bed on the plastic couch. Lexi climbed into her hospital bed and arranged the pillows and blankets she had brought from home. The plastic mattress squeaked with her every move. She settled into a comfortable position and began scrolling through her phone.

"I found him on Instagram," Lexi said, a few minutes later.

"Found who?" Emily responded.

"Ricky Stafford, the guy from the clinic with the hair," she replied with a practiced nonchalance. "Should I follow him?"

"If you want to," said Emily as she opened the cupboard door to unpack the snacks they had brought from home. The hospital had snacks, but there were certain ones that Lexi tolerated better than others. Lexi caught a glimpse of her favorite popcorn and made a mental note. She needed to try to eat that before the inevitable mouth sores made their appearance.

"He seemed really nice, and it would be cool to know another teenager that has gone through cancer," Emily said, as she busied herself unpacking their movie collection.

"What if he thinks I'm some kind of stalker or super weird for just randomly following him?" Lexi asked. "He probably doesn't even remember who I am."

Emily delighted in the fact that Lexi had something other than the impending treatment to focus on.

"Twenty seconds of courage, sis. That's all it takes. Just do it and see what happens," Emily replied, fully aware that Lexi was drawn to this boy for more than just a supportive voice. "Plus, you are kind of a stalker," she added with a laugh.

The nurses busied themselves around Lexi like bees around a hive. They buzzed back and forth preparing the tubing, saline, and multiple medications that would tether Lexi to her pumps for the next several weeks. Emily continued with the unpacking of her bottomless bag. Lexi took in the scene around her. For the next month she would be surrounded by these four blue walls. This was her personal containment chamber. It may be filled with friendly faces, and nail polish, face masks and gel pens, but in her heart Lexi knew she couldn't leave until the doctors said she could. She was trapped. Her world instantly felt smaller in that moment and she willed her chemo-battered lungs to take a deep breath.

Lexi picked up her phone with determination. She opened Instagram and clicked on the search tab. She typed in the letter "R" and Ricky's name came up. He was the last person she had searched. She was hoping her low blood counts would keep her face from flushing at the knowledge. She clicked on his profile and then tapped the "follow" button.

"I did it—aah!" Lexi squealed in triumph. The rush of adrenaline from doing something so outside of her comfort zone was akin to Red Bull being pumped straight into her central line. Her heart beat rapidly and she was grateful that she wasn't due for another set of vitals for thirty minutes. Emily smiled and gave a short laugh at the effect this boy was having on her daughter after just one chance interaction. Not five minutes had passed, and the endless unpacking was interrupted once again.

"He followed me back, Mom! What do I do now?" Lexi said in a slight panic. "I wanna message him but I don't want to sound like a creep. What should I say?"

Lexi had often been told that she was not a "typical" teenage girl. The thought made her smile now. Was there even such a thing as "typical"? Her long dark brown hair, coupled with her clear blue eyes had made certain that she didn't go unnoticed by the opposite sex. However, she had not ever focused much on the way she looked. Likewise, she found herself drawn to the type of boys that took the time to focus on character rather than superficial things. She wasn't exactly sure which type of boy Ricky was yet, but she was interested in finding out. The fact that he had cancer and by default could relate to her in a way that not many people could was reason enough to get to know him better.

"Hmmm," said Emily out loud, relishing the excitement in her daughter's eyes as they talked about Ricky. She took an exaggerated breath in and exhaled slowly as if she was putting all of her brain power into this project. "Maybe start with 'Hey!'" she said with playful sarcasm.

"Obviously," Lexi said with a laugh as she mockingly rolled her eyes and sent the initial message. Emily picked up a dry erase marker and opened the worn-out scriptures she had pulled out of the bag.

"Mom! Help!"

The panic in Lexi's voice caused Emily to turn to face her. Lexi was staring at her phone with mock concern. Emily's face responded back in confusion.

"He replied! I'm freaking out a little," Lexi said excitedly.

Emily tried to hide the small laugh that was threatening to escape as she watched her daughter fret over a response. She was grateful for this normal glimpse into teenage social life that Lexi rarely experienced these days.

"What are you going to say now?" Emily asked, matching Lexi's enthusiasm.

"I don't even know . . ." Lexi said as she exhaled. Her drawn on brows furrowed as she pondered on what every teen knows is clearly a life altering decision—How do I respond when the opposite sex asks, *What are you doing?*

Just then her nurse came in with the first dose of her transplant chemo. Lexi quickly caught the nurse up on the dilemma she was facing. The nurse's eyes lit up with excitement and her face glowed with anticipation. She quickly joined in the conversation, asking all of the appropriate questions that any girl would ask when their friend was texting a guy for the first time: "How did you guys meet? Is he funny? What does he look like? Do you like him?" At that moment Lexi was transported from her containment chamber to a normal room, where people talked about normal things. She felt almost like a normal teenage girl, just having a conversation about a normal teenage boy, with her normal friends.

The pump beeped, indicating air in the line. The fact that Lexi no longer lived in a normal world crashed around her. The rubble felt tangible. The nurse dutifully went to work silencing the pump and fixing the occlusion. The chemo continued its unimpeded course from the bag on Lexi's IV pole to her veins once again. But, she wasn't willing to let go of her sense of normalcy just yet. If she was going to make her move, she had to do it now. The phone was growing heavier in her thin hands. Her long fingers worked to keep the device balanced as her thumb tapped the bottom of the screen in hopes of drumming up a response before her eyelids grew too heavy.

With determination Lexi looked at Emily and said, "I'm just going to say, 'not much' and then ask if he ever had to have radiation."

"Wow," Emily said with a semi-concerned face. "Your pickup game might need a little work." Lexi feigned offense and they both laughed.

Lexi shrugged her shoulders and raised her faux brows in concentration. She focused on tapping her phone screen in the correct place to formulate a legible message. Her head hurt with effort as she focused on the important task. She read the short message through once before hitting send. She had been known to text gibberish a time or two during treatment and she didn't want to make the same error with someone she barely knew. Lexi laid her head back on the thin hospital pillow, entirely exhausted by the rush of endorphins that accompanies every text a teenage girl sends a cute boy. She put her phone in the basket of the IV pole she was chained to and drifted off to sleep. The fatal chemo slowly trickled into her veins and a thick fog clouded her brain. The poisonous liquid would reveal its most horrifying effects in the years to come.

Time is merely a word when you are going through treatment for cancer. Some days last forever, dragging a person behind them as a wounded soldier drags a useless limb through battle. Other days, a patient is barely lucid enough to remember the passage of time; eyelids are too heavy to open, limbs too heavy to function, and a mind too cloudy to command response. Each day for the next week Lexi received a cocktail of high dose chemo infusions that knocked her body lower than she realized was physically possible. She had experienced the poison before, but this was beyond brutal. Lexi's eyes groggily worked to focus on the scripture Emily had written on her whiteboard. "For I reckon that the sufferings of this present time are not worthy to be compared with the glory which shall be revealed in us. —Romans 8:18". The words allowed Lexi to breathe beyond the blue walls. Yes, she was suffering now, but she would not suffer forever. Better days were ahead.

Lexi's ligaments rippled across her back as she lurched forward to vomit again, unable to do so. She had been unable to eat for days now and had long since expelled any stomach acid she had accrued. The blue hospital bag crinkled in her long fingers, and she wiped at the corners of her swollen mouth gently. The mouth sores had begun a few days ago. She could feel the burn of the trail they left in their wake, as if the top layer of her skin had been removed leaving the nerve endings exposed. Only this time, the mouth sores hadn't stopped in her mouth. She'd overheard her doctor tell Emily during morning rounds that the sores had traveled into Lexi's ear canal and down the length of her GI tract.

"This is the worst case I've seen in the fifteen years I've been here," the doctor said under a furrowed brow. "Poor girl. They will go away when her counts come up, but that depends on how fast her body heals itself and, if I'm being completely honest, her body wasn't doing well before we started this transplant. In the meantime, all we can do is try the numbing mouthwash and hope to see some improvement quickly. Pain medication doesn't even touch these things."

Lexi's daily routine consisted of small tasks that felt insurmountable given the allotment of energy her body now required just to sit up. Among the mundane tasks, Lexi was required to shower and change into a fresh hospital gown every four hours. This procedure was meant to keep the chemo from leaving literal burns on her fair skin as her body secreted the toxins through her pores. Despite her complete exhaustion, she remained committed to the monotonous protocol. Unfortunately, Lexi would not be spared the horrid burns.

The hours Lexi spent awake became fewer and farther between. The muscle fibers in her body felt as if they were elastics that had been pulled too tight and were just waiting to snap. Her bones held the ache of a rigid screen door during a windstorm. The four walls of the hospital room grew smaller with each passing day; sky blue barriers that kept her locked away from the rest of the world and with it, any hope of a normal life.

The day of transplant finally arrived. Labeling it as anticlimactic would've been a gross understatement, not that she was looking for excitement those days. The type of excitement that the hospital held usually involved beeping monitors, codes being disconcertingly announced over the speakers, too many worried faces, and a stay in the ICU. Lexi was good with anticlimactic.

Kris, Lexi's dad, sat on the couch in her room. His signature baseball cap was perched atop his head, covering his tawny curls. His face reflected the normal conversational responses when someone spoke to him, but anyone who knew him could see the brokenness of the innermost parts of his soul just by looking into his blue eyes. Lexi's youngest sister, Aleah, was sitting on Kris's lap asking curiously about each machine and medication that her sister was hooked up to. Her brown hair was pulled into a side ponytail that tried, unsuccessfully, to smooth the tight curls that escaped around her face. Her blue eyes swirled with wonder and dread about the concoctions she was seeing, as her heart tried to wrap around what was happening to her big sister.

Liv, at ten, was just two years older than Aleah and five years younger than Lexi. She had gone from being one of "The Littles" in the family, to becoming the oldest sister at home, overnight. Liv's long blonde hair was pulled into a low bun—one of the only hairstyles she had recently mastered. Her green eyes and playful freckles yearned for adventure, but her heart was tethered to her family's pain. Without a word she began learning how to do Aleah's hair for school and making sure her youngest sister was doing okay throughout the day. Liv cuddled quietly next to Lexi's side, taking note that hospital beds were not as comfortable as her bed at home was.

Cam, the only brother in the Gould family, was on a stool, as always, not far from his big sister. Cam and Lexi had grown up telling everyone they were twins and most people believed it. They both sported chestnut hair with light eyes. While Lexi's eyes could not be described by any color other than blue, Cam's eyes held a hint of green that accompanied his mischievous nature. Although Cam was two years younger than Lexi, they had appeared the same age for most of their lives and the bond they shared was palpable.

Lexi's doctors entered the room along with the child life specialist who looked entirely too excited for the circumstances. Family and medical staff alike gathered around Lexi's hospital bed and began to sing "Happy BMT Birthday to You!" The song was sung in the same tune as the original, with all of the same lyrics. The only difference was that everyone tried to awkwardly squish "BMT" (short for Bone Marrow Transplant) in between "Happy" and "Birthday." While "Happy Birthday" seemed like an odd choice to sing before a stem cell transplant, it was ironically accurate. Lexi's body would have to completely rebuild itself. Her cells would all be new. She would even need to get all of her immunizations again. At the conclusion of the song, Lexi's nurse carried her stem-cells in an IV bag and hung it on her pole. The long tubing from the bag was connected to one of the many tubes protruding from Lexi's body. The nurse checked and rechecked that all of the connections were secure and the took a step back.

The cells slowly dripped from the bag, down the tubing, and into Lexi's veins via the central line. The smell of creamed corn filled the room and Lexi vowed to never eat that yellow mush again. There was no pump this time, these cells were too precious to force into the body and risk losing any of them in the process. Gravity and time were the only form of transportation this infusion needed. Lexi lay in her bed and tried to think of something other than creamed corn.

Over the following days Lexi spent her time alternating between the standard, hospital issued blue plastic vomit bags, and trying to sleep. She focused all of her energy on nothing more than willing her stem cells to work faster so that her mouth sores would clear up. She was hoping that the process would help her bones quit aching, and her body begin to heal. Despite the long days, a part of Lexi couldn't help but check her phone every now and then.

As Lexi's frail hands picked up the gadget that seemed heavier than it had been only two short weeks ago, she read the latest Instagram message from Ricky.

"He asked for my number because it is easier for us to text than to message over Instagram," Lexi said sheepishly to Emily. Lexi's face had become swollen as a result of the chemo-induced mouth sores, but that didn't stop an *I told you so grin* from trying to reach her puffy eyes. "I guess my pick-up game is a little stronger than you thought, huh?" She wiggled the bald skin above her eyes where her eyebrows should have been. Emily just shook her head and laughed.

Later that night as she was getting ready for bed, Lexi's phone buzzed indicating a text. It had now been just over a month since she had first met Ricky in the clinic and they had stayed in touch ever since. They did not talk consistently throughout the day. Lexi did not have the energy to keep up on social relationships that way, but Ricky understood. He would send her a message and she would text back when she had the strength and the energy to do so. Sometimes it took her days to reply and other times she could reply in minutes. Regardless of her reaction time, she never got the feeling that Ricky was bothered by her lack of social norms. A small seed of hope formed in the very bottom of her heart at the thought that perhaps he really did understand what she was going through. She picked up her phone and read the text.

"He said he remembers how boring it was in the hospital and asked if I wanted a friend to come keep me company for a bit. Do you care if he comes up tomorrow?" Lexi asked Emily, hoping that the warmth rushing to her cheeks could be concealed as a reaction to the blood transfusion she'd received earlier in the day.

"I think that sounds fun," replied Emily. "I can go down to the cafeteria when he gets here and get you guys some snacks when I grab my dinner. How does that sound?"

"That would be great," said Lexi. "I hope it's not weird when he gets here. We've been talking a lot but some guys are just different in person."

"I get the feeling that Ricky is pretty comfortable in his own skin. I think he'll be just fine, and you guys will have fun. You can play games or something. Just go easy on him. You can be intimidating," Emily said, smiling.

"I'm fifteen. I have no eyelashes and I'm completely bald," Lexi replied matter-of-factly. "Some days I can't even walk by myself. There is nothing intimidating about me."

"Strong, beautiful girls can always be intimidating to teenage boys—even when they don't have eyelashes," countered Emily.

"Most days I can't even open my own water bottle, Mom. I haven't been strong for a long time now. The beautiful part? Well, let's just say that I think he's coming up to visit because he is a nice guy and I'm a kid with cancer." Before Emily could offer a rebuttal, Lexi added, "Besides, cancer is ugly, Mom. I wouldn't ever put someone through this life. Anyway, I don't need to worry about anything like that with Ricky," she said dismissively. "For now, I just need to decide which one of my nightgowns is the cutest and make sure my eyebrows don't rub off on the pillow before he gets here. It's not every day that I get a new visitor."

Ricky walked through the double doors of the hospital and his long legs made light work of the four flights of stairs that led to the ICS floor. He strolled along with ease and noticed that his body was getting stronger the longer he was off chemo. He easily reached the automated doors that led to the ICS clinic. The doors opened with the push of a button and Ricky's mind opened up to the recollection of how hard treatment really had been. The aroma of sanitizer triggered the fear he'd experienced when he was first diagnosed. The crinkle of those wretched blue vomit bags as they were pulled from their place on the wall caused his skin to subconsciously crawl from the effects the chemo had on him. The time he'd spent away from his family and the guilt of feeling that somehow it was all his fault topped off the emotional downpour. Ricky quickly sidestepped it before being swept away in its current. Those were murky waters he knew he couldn't swim in. His heart rate escalated ever so slightly as he neared the room that Lexi had said she was staying in. An odd sense of déjà vu made his stomach turn as he realized that it was right next to his original diagnosis room. Emotions worked their strange ebb and flow once again. Ricky took a purposeful breath to keep them at bay. He focused on reminding himself that he was wearing a visitor's badge instead of a patient bracelet this time. The thought made taking another breath just a little easier.

Ricky took in his surroundings. The inpatient scene really hadn't changed much in the last few years. Some of the nurses were the same. However, some were not. That part wasn't a surprise. This was a hard job with a hard reality. Not every story ended like his did. Without warning, his mind shifted from cancer to his new cancer friend. He allowed his psyche to drift for the slightest moment as he got up the courage to knock on her door.

From the moment that he met her, there was something in Lexi's eyes that spoke volumes without her saying a word. She possessed raw beauty unlike anything he had ever seen. She didn't need all of the extra stuff that the other girls used to be attractive, and that made her more lovely. Something about her said that she was who she was, without apology. She stood out in ways he never imagined possible. If he were being honest, that made him more nervous than he wanted to admit. People were clearly taken with Lexi, yet she did not ask for attention. He knew he was drawn to her and wanted to be around her, but wasn't quite sure why. For now he would admit to only one thing—she needed a friend and he took pride in being a good one.

Cancer life was lonely, especially for a teenager. It seemed to be either feast or famine in the social department. He remembered it like it was yesterday: being diagnosed and everyone wanting to be around and visit. Then, as time went on and you got too sick to respond to texts and messages, people faded away. It wasn't their fault, life went on and you just weren't a part of it. To be fair, by the time this happened you were likely so sick and exhausted from treatment that you didn't have the energy to realize you were missing out. It ended up being an odd sort of blessing.

He dismissed all of the thoughts he had been using as a distraction, took a breath, and knocked on the heavy wooden door to Lexi's room. Emily answered and greeted him warmly. He quickly caught sight of Lexi in her hospital bed, multiple tubes acting as intricate subways for the medication she needed to be delivered directly to her veins. To his surprise, she looked frailer than the day they'd met in clinic, her bones somewhat more prominent through her perfect complexion. Ricky knew she was in the hospital for her first stem cell transplant. Although he was lucky enough to have avoided that during his own cancer treatment, he had heard stories of what transplant entailed. None of them were good.

Ricky's eyes met Lexi's and he noticed that despite the physical impact the transplant had on her body, the light in her sapphire eyes was miraculously unscathed. Upon seeing him she instantly smiled, and it seemed to immediately melt any feeling of uneasiness he might have been harboring.

"Hey!" she said.

"Hey!" he responded with a grin. "I brought you the blue bug juice you said you liked. They're a lot harder to find than I thought. It might have been a little easier if I would've known what I was looking for, but I've never even heard of these things. Are they really any good?"

"You've never had them?" Lexi said in disbelief. "They are the best! They taste like melted blue popsicles. You really didn't have to bring me anything though, but thank you," she said with a warm smile that reached her eyes. He returned the gesture and wondered to himself if there was anyone anywhere that didn't smile when Lexi smiled. He didn't see how it would've been possible.

"I know what it's like to not have an appetite, so when we were texting and you said you were craving one of those things, I knew I had to find you one and bring it up," Ricky said, as he took a seat on the chair next to Lexi's bed.

The next few hours were spent laughing and playing card games. Nurses came in and out of the room to check Lexi's vitals, give her transfusions, administer medications, and begin her IV nutrition. Ricky noticed how Lexi greeted each one of her nurses and techs by name as if they were old friends. Lexi liked how Ricky hid behind the door when he saw the nurses coming to try to scare them and make her laugh. He didn't seem bothered by the fact that she had tubes going in her body or that the two of them had to move her IV pole around if they wanted to watch TV. Being together was just easy and they both felt it.

"Well Lex, it looks like your meds are really starting to kick in and I should probably be getting home. I promised my parents I would be home by midnight.," Ricky said as he stood and stretched his long legs.

"Thank you again for coming all the way up to see me," Lexi said sleepily. Their visit had left Lexi's heart full but her body completely worn out. "And thanks again for the bug juice. I still can't believe you brought me that." The small sentiment carried a deeper understanding than her words could express, but somehow he seemed to understand the gratitude she was trying to convey.

"Chemo is not fun. I'm just glad that those still sound good and that I found them. I only had to stop at five stores, but it was worth it," he teased.

"Ricky," Lex said, shaking her weary head, "you really didn't have to."

"I know, but I wanted to because I knew it would make you smile." His words caused the small seed in Lexi's heart to take root as he added, "Thanks for letting me come visit, Lex."

"Thanks for coming up," Lexi said. "You make the hospital a lot more fun."

"Does that mean you'll let me come up again?" Ricky said with a wiggle of his genuine eyebrows.

"Yes, but bring your A-game because I'm going to beat you in Phase 10 again," Lexi responded with a challenge.

Ricky laughed as he hugged her goodbye and told her he would text her the following day. Lexi told him to drive safe and he smiled that she was that kind of person—of course she was. He easily walked down the four flights of stairs and strolled through the double doors of the hospital to his car. The corners of his mouth involuntarily turned upwards the entirety of the forty-five-minute drive home and he couldn't exactly understand why. He had just gone and visited someone at the hospital. He was a caring guy—it was in his nature to think of others. Surely that was his only motivation in going to see Lexi tonight . . . and in wanting to go back to visit her again soon.

Chapter 3

*"Sometimes someone comes into your life, so unexpect-
edly, takes your heart by surprise, and changes your life
forever." —Unknown*

Shortly after Ricky left, Lexi and Emily began their bedtime routine. Transplant protocol required that certain procedures be followed every night and a social life was no exception to these rules.
Lexi sleepily complied as Emily assisted her from one task to the next.
Her eyelids hung heavily and her feet shuffled as she willed herself into
completing each duty the best that her worn-out body would allow.

Occasionally, Lexi would pause to catch her breath and reiterate
something funny that Ricky had done or said during their visit. Emily
recalled each piece of conversation Lexi shared but loved reliving
something other than cancer treatments. More than that, it warmed
Emily's heart to see Lexi's face as she spoke about her new friend. The
recollection of her visit with Ricky brought a sparkle to Lexi's eyes
that even anti-nausea medication couldn't dull.

The week passed and the debilitating effects of the transplant
chemo blossomed into a dark reality. Lexi's body sunk to a new low
as she fought through treatment. Her muscles groaned in protest as
she pushed herself through each nightly task after spending each day
convincing her body to survive. Her phone intermittently lit up with
a text from Ricky like a lighthouse in a storm. At times she was able
to respond, other times she had only the energy to read what he wrote
before her body required more rest. Ricky was patient, undeterred,

and unbothered. It became his mission to bring a smile to Lexi's face despite her undesirable circumstances. He knew that the world needed her smile, and something inside of him said that he needed it too.

The sound of Lexi's voice broke through the humming of the monitors she was tethered to. "Mom," she said through swollen cheeks, "if I am not awake, can you ask the Art Lady for some paper and some colored pencils next time she stops by?" Conversation had been limited for Lexi these days, due to the pain that accompanied it. The sores in her mouth had continued their unrelenting rampage. While limiting the movement of her mouth did not take the pain away, it kept her mouth from being further aggravated by unnecessary activity.

"I'm sure she has some," Emily said, surprised that Lexi would suddenly feel up to drawing when she had barely been demonstrating the energy to sit up by herself the last week. "Are you making a card for someone?" Lexi had a tendency to meet new friends in the hospital as well as the clinic. Oftentimes, she would use her limited energy to make someone a card, a poster, or a craft in an effort to brighten their day.

Trying her best to smile through a puffy face, Lexi responded slowly, the newly administered pain medication causing her speech to slur slightly. "Ricky plays the ukulele. He said that he would come play for me and we could sing together. I told him I couldn't sing right now, so he told me that I had to draw him a picture instead." She rested her eyelids for a long moment before continuing, the energy of the conversation taking its toll. "He's on vacation visiting his cousins in Washington for about a week, but it's going to take me a while to have enough strength to draw a whole picture so I should get started." Lexi exhaled and replaced the ice packs on either side of her mouth. The strings of each ice pack had been tied together on one end. The tied ends were swathed over her bald head to allow the ice packs to drape her distended cheeks like awkwardly placed window coverings. The strategically placed apparatus was used in an effort to try to numb the pain in her mouth. With great effort, she once again found the most tolerable position in the uncomfortable hospital bed and drifted off to sleep, completely worn out from the energy expounded by the brief interaction.

Lexi was an artist in her own rite, her medium being her body as she freely danced. She could create beautiful movement and choreograph works of art that spoke to others without saying a word. However, her artistic ability in dance did not transfer to the art of drawing. The fact that she was being given enough Dilaudid to make a grown man twirl around in a tutu only added to her lack of sketching ability. Yet Lexi was determined to give it her all. Over the course of the next few days, she used her small bouts of energy to hold her phone and look up pictures of cartoon dinosaurs.

"What about this one, mom?" Lexi asked Emily after trying unsuccessfully to focus on her phone screen. "This looks like a pretty easy one to draw, right?" Lexi had found a brachiosaurus, or long neck dinosaur, with very little detail surrounding it. "Yeah, that looks good," Emily said. "You can definitely draw that—even while you're on your meds."

"Okay, good. I'll start tomorrow," Lexi said, as she put her phone back in her IV pole. She closed her eyes and worked to drown out the low humming of the pump that she was shackled to. She focused on the rise and fall of her chest. With each breath came the forced effort of inhaling and exhaling. In and out. Breathing should be relaxing, she thought, a way to escape these four blue walls. Instead, even her lungs seemed to be turning against her. She had been in the hospital for three weeks now and she'd remain inpatient until her body recovered from the transplant enough that it was safe for her to go back home. She'd be able to sleep in her own bed again for a couple weeks and then she'd be back up here to do all of this again. Thinking about what was to come wouldn't help her breathe any easier tonight.

Emily's phone buzzed and she glanced down at the message. It had been a few days since Lexi had heard from Ricky but she knew he had been on vacation and was likely just busy hanging out with his family. If she had the opportunity, she'd be doing the exact same thing.

Emily glanced down to see who the message was from and read it aloud. "Ricky wanted me to write and ask how Lexi is doing," the text from Maren began. "His phone gave up the ghost." A soft smile played at the corners of Lexi's mouth at the mention that Ricky was concerned with how she was doing. Emily's phone dinged a second time. She climbed onto Lexi's bed so they could view the message together. This time it was a video of Ricky at the beach holding perfectly still while his younger brother, Abe, held a crawdad to his chest.

Maren had taken the liberty of slowing the video down so that every bit of unfiltered anguish was evident on Ricky's face as the crawdad got just close enough to pinch Ricky's skin, causing Abe to squeal with delight. The four blue walls seemed to disappear as the humming of the pumps were replaced with Lexi's giggles. She couldn't help but replay the video half a dozen times, holding her aching cheeks and laughing unrestrained each time. Emily updated Ricky via Maren on Lexi's condition and set up a time for Ricky to come visit the day after he returned from vacation.

Hospital life was pretty monotonous for the most part. The nurses did their best to spread cheer and Emily was always trying to find ways to make the time go quicker. But there was something about when Ricky came to visit that made the hospital just a little more tolerable. Lexi wasn't sure if it was the effects of her most recent medication or the knowledge that she would see Ricky soon, but something was causing her stomach to feel as if a hive of bees were swarming around an open can of soda in the middle of summer. However, she knew that she needed to be practical. If she used all of her energy to be excited to hang out with Ricky, she would be feeling horrible and would likely not have the strength to visit with him when he actually got there later that day. She had to find a way to calm down and get some rest before he came up.

"Mom," Lexi said. "Ricky is coming up but I'm going to try to sleep before he gets here. Will you just do me a favor and make sure that if one of my eyebrows comes off during my nap that you draw it back on before he comes in?" Emily assured Lexi that both of her brows would be on point for her visitor. "Will you also, make sure my hair isn't sticking up?" Lexi said as she patted her smooth scalp and wiggled her stenciled brows. Upon Emily's assuredness that Lexi would be as prepared for her visitor as possible, Lexi allowed her eyelids a break from the stress of staying open.

With ukulele in hand, Ricky headed through the double doors of the hospital and his thoughts instantly turned to Lexi. This wasn't uncommon, the more he interacted with Lexi, the more he craved her presence in his life. But it wasn't just her that he had begun to see differently. He began to see himself differently. His confidence waning somewhat, he began to question himself. Were his standards what they really needed to be? Was he focused on the things he needed to focus on? His whole life he had valued what others thought, doing his best to fit in with whomever he was around. He wanted, needed, to be liked by others. His physical appearance and physical abilities were inseparably linked with his self-worth. However, that was beginning to change. His focus was beginning to change. When Lexi spoke of someone, she rarely mentioned their physical attributes, instead she spoke of their character. Ricky could not help but wonder what she thought of his character. Did she ever look at him the way he hoped she one day would? Or did she see him as ordinary as he now saw other girls? He wanted to stand out to her, to be special to her the way she was quickly becoming to him. Since they had begun talking more regularly he had tried his hand at flirting with her, but she mildly played it off. No doubt she had already heard every pick up line; no doubt she had not fallen for any of them. It was clear from the first time he looked into her blue eyes that there was something distinct about this girl, and that fact had only grown more evident the more he got to know her. Ricky understood what to say to get a girl's attention, how to flatter her to make her fall for him. But, he knew those tools would be useless in this endeavor.

Ricky's long legs carried him easily up the stairs. He swiped the badge that gave him access to the fourth-floor cancer unit and sanitized his hands as he began walking towards Lexi's room. He willed the butterflies in his stomach to stop doing backflips and hoped that his confident swagger could cover the slight shaking in his limbs that he tried to control when he was around Lexi. He still hadn't quite gotten used to the effect her presence had on him. He had come to terms with the fact that he likely had a crush on her, but generally when he had a crush he felt a little more confident in himself and his abilities to be funny or at least know what to say. Ricky had the ability to be fluid, to become whomever he needed to be to capture a heart, but somehow Lexi saw through all of that. She made him feel as if he had nothing to prove, as if he was enough. Yet, somehow she also challenged him to want to be better in every aspect of his life. Who knew a bald girl with no eyelashes could have such an impact on him?

Ricky noticed the smile and whisperings of the nurses outside of Lexi's room as they greeted him. He held up the small string instrument he'd been carrying in his right hand.

"Do you think if I play the ukulele for Lex, she'll fall in love with me?" he asked as he flashed them a quick smile. By now all of the nurses on the floor were well aware of who Ricky Stafford was—even the ones who had not taken care of him personally. He was the handsome boy who had come up and played games with Lexi. He was the boy that told jokes just to watch her laugh. The boy that beat cancer but drove almost an hour to visit a friend in the cancer unit.

The group of nurses giggled good-naturedly at his endless confidence. "Good luck with that, Ricky. Lexi isn't just another teenage girl. You're going to have to work a lot harder for her," one of the nurses said laughing.

"Let us know how it goes," another said with a playful smile.

"It can't hurt though, right?" Ricky replied, knowing all too well that they were right. This was going to take some effort on his part. He knocked on Lexi's door and waited a moment for Emily to answer. She opened it and warmly greeted him. Lex was sitting in the bed with a sleepy smile looking like she had just woken up. She noticed the uke in his hand and instantly lit up. Lexi's face was a bit rounder than the last time he had come to visit. Her skin looked paler with a yellow undertone. Her eyes shone bright, just as he had remembered them, but there were now dark half-moons under each one.

"You brought it!" Lexi said. "What are you going to play for me?" She looked at him as if he held the answers to the world's problems in his hands. She'd never even heard him sing, yet he could see in her eyes that she believed he would make life better just by serenading her.

"Hold up," Ricky said with a tease in his voice. "We had a deal. Remember?" He did his best to set his jaw and look as stern as he could muster. He hoped she wouldn't challenge him. He could already feel his defenses weakening. Who was he kidding? He would sing to this girl every day if she would let him. Lexi raised her fake eyebrows and her forehead wrinkles climbed up to where her hairline should have started. She held up her hands in preparation to explain her drawing.

"Well, I do remember actually. Before you see my drawing, you should just know that I warned you that I am not a very good artist and that they do have me on a lot of medication. But, I did work very hard on it for you." She looked very proud of herself as she added, "Also, I labeled everything in the drawing just in case you couldn't tell what it was."

At that, Ricky could no longer contain himself and he broke into a smile. He walked over to her bed to see the Alexis Gould original. The masterpiece featured a simple, yet identifiable long neck dinosaur. Riding on top of the dinosaur, was a stick figure with spiky hair and an arrow pointing to it that said "Ricky." The masterpiece was made complete with flowers, a sun, clouds, and patches of grass. Each item was, in fact, labeled. Just in case.

"This is too great!" Ricky said excitedly.

"You can be honest," Lexi replied. "It's probably the best picture of you riding a dinosaur that you've ever had drawn for you, isn't it?"

"Pretty much!" he said.

Lex shrugged her shoulders as if she had not used all of her energy of the last week creating the simple drawing. "I knew it. Okay, now it's your turn," she said while motioning to the ukulele.

Ricky sat on the stool next to her bed and began. The lyrics to Jeremy Passion's soft ballad "Lemonade" filled the room.

> *She's my sunshine in the rain*
> *My Tylenol when I'm in pain, yeah*
> *Let me tell you what she means to me*
> *Like a tall glass of lemonade*
> *When it's burning hot on summer days*
> *She's exactly what I need*

Ricky's voice was clearer than Lexi expected but not overpowering. His confidence carried over to his musical talents in a good way. There was no bravado when he sang, no need to impress anyone. There was only Ricky, his ukulele, and a piece of his heart that Lexi felt he must save for his music. Knowing that he chose to come to the hospital to share this part of himself with her caused the small seed in her heart to sprout.

Ricky had quickly become a constant in Lexi's life. It was unusual for Lexi to have a feeling like this so quickly. She had always considered herself in control of her emotions— guarded even. Since being diagnosed, she had unintentionally built a wall to protect herself from being hurt. Four blue walls to be precise. Afterall, who would fall for the bald girl with no eyelashes? Yet somehow Ricky seemed to look at those walls, smile at them, and with ukulele in tow, climb right over and make Lexi feel completely at ease.

Chapter 4

*"You can take your 'I'm okay' hat off now. It's just me.
Fall apart. I'm not going anywhere."—Erin Van Vuren*

Blue skies beat blue walls any day, Lexi thought as she felt the warm sun on her bald head. She waited curbside in her wheelchair for Emily to bring the van up. The wind blew slightly, and the nurse instinctively adjusted the blanket that lay across Lexi's lap. Lexi smiled at the gesture, but more so at the sensation. It wasn't every day that she had the blessing of feeling a fresh breeze on her face. She'd been in the hospital for just over a month, but today she was finally going home.

The white minivan rolled to a stop just in front of the hospital double doors and Emily quickly put the vehicle in park and jumped out. The nurse opened the front door and Lexi gingerly stood as she grasped Emily's arm for support. Quickly and efficiently, the nurse moved the pancaked hospital pillows from Lexi's wheelchair to her seat in the van in hopes they would provide some sort of comfort for the ride. The nurse gently closed the door and waved goodbye as the van pulled away from the curb and headed towards Lexi's favorite destination: home.

The enthusiastic energy surrounding Lexi's heart seemed to flow freely from her transplant riddled body. It made a conscious effort to infect Emily as well and was welcomed in its attack.

"Mom, can we get treats and have a family movie night while we're at home?" Lexi asked. Her appetite had abandoned her months ago, but the knowledge that she only had a few short weeks to make memories with her family before another month-long hospital stay could not be ignored. She cleared the impending treatment from her psyche and willed the knowledge to stay far from her mind. For today, she would focus only on how grateful she was for what was right in front of her. Her limbs weighed heavy with exerted exhaustion, but her mind felt more alive than it had in weeks.

"Of course!" Emily responded. "We can plan a day when you feel up to walking around the store and we can all go pick out our favorite treat. Then you guys can make a big bed on the couch and have a sibling sleepover. It will be just like old times." Emily had begun the sentence with enthusiasm, but Lexi sensed the melancholy note on which it ended. She looked over to see the smile that didn't fully reach Emily's green eyes. Lexi didn't ask why. She didn't have to. They both knew that life would never again be "just like old times."

They could have family movie nights, they could buy treats, and build forts, and big beds, and giggle for hours. But under the laughter lay the fear of what their reality was. In addition to the movies, treats, laughter, and piles of blankets strewn about, there would also be nightly meds, a blue plastic bag in case she got sick, Lexi's pole for her IV nutrition, and a thermometer just for good measure. They learned long ago not to waste their days yearning for life before cancer. They would seize the day and appreciate the precious time they were given. Yet, on occasion a fond memory of life before diagnosis crept into recollection and tugged at the heart like a puppeteer choosing which emotional string to play with.

The three weeks at home were cherished and filled with absolutely everything and nothing all at once. Each mundane task was considered extraordinary. Lexi could walk freely from room to room, her feet feeling the warm carpeted floor of her bedroom or the cool laminate of her kitchen. She could sit on a couch that didn't smell like bleach and cuddle up next to her siblings every night while watching TV, without someone coming in every thirty minutes to check her vitals. She could wear regular bracelets that dangled when she walked instead of a hospital bracelet that said her name and identification number for transfusions. Lexi wondered how many people took for granted the magic of these menial occurrences in their everyday lives. If it weren't for cancer, would she have fallen victim to the same attitude? The thought made her grateful in a strange sense for this terrible disease. It was an odd feeling—finding gratitude in the situation that could be the end of your life. Perhaps the change of perspective was something good that would come of all of the baldness.

The precious time at home passed far too quickly and Lexi soon found herself in the white minivan heading back to the confinement of the four blue walls. Bile rose in her throat as the recollection of her previous transplant all but consumed her. She was stronger than she had been just a few weeks ago when she was discharged from her first transplant, but she was nowhere near healthy. How could she possibly survive another transplant so quickly? She understood far too well that there were things worse than death.

"Hey Lex, good luck this week! You're heading in for your second transplant, right?" Ricky's text pulled Lexi from her thoughts and back to reality. She smiled subconsciously as she reread his text. With everything that Ricky had going on in his life, he still had a way of making her feel like he cared about what was happening in hers. With the smile never leaving her face, Lexi placed the phone in her lap, securing it under her hands like a secret treasure she wasn't yet ready to share with the world. She made the decision to wait until she was settled into her hospital room before texting him back. It would give her something to look forward to, rather than focusing on the upcoming transplant and the new pain that she'd been trying to ignore that had begun creeping in on the left side of her abdomen.

Emily found a spot in the front of the hospital parking lot marked "Transplant Patient" and slowly turned in. The van came to a stop and Lex involuntarily winced as she braced her left side. *Breathe.* She told herself. She wanted to believe that the stabbing in her side was nothing more than a reaction to being back at the hospital for another transplant—a physical assault from anxiety brought on by what she'd already endured and what was yet to come. In her heart she knew this wasn't true. The intense throbbing had begun earlier that morning and had consistently gotten worse with each passing hour.

"Who says there aren't any perks to getting a transplant?" Emily said, as she motioned to the designated parking sign. Lexi gave a small laugh and intuitively pulled her hand tighter to offer her abdomen more support. The movement was not lost on Emily. The lightheartedness of her demeanor vacated abruptly. Emily's eyes quickly darted from Lexi's hand back to her face in an effort to gauge the amount of pain that Lexi was in. Lexi gave a wan smile in a feeble attempt at warding off Emily's worry.

"Let's go get you settled, and I'll come back for the rest of our stuff," Emily said quickly, hoping to mask her concern. She matched Lexi's painted-on smile, but the unspoken truth had been felt by both of them. Something wasn't right.

As they exited the van, they began the slow trek across the parking lot and through the double doors, Lexi could feel that although she was stronger than she'd been a few weeks ago, her body was far weaker than it had been just six weeks ago. It wasn't the kind of weakness you experience from a really great workout; Lexi knew that kind of weakness and her body yearned to feel that way again. This was a type of fragility that went beyond her muscles—deep into her bones. It was as if she could feel her marrow fighting to survive while her nerves screamed in agony. It was not a pleasant process.

Lexi walked with great effort. *One foot in front of the other,* she thought as she shuffled alongside Emily. Emily was usually a fast-paced walker, a side effect of being the shortest in her family. The speed Lexi was going must've been like nails on a chalkboard to her, but she didn't let on. Emily just stayed by her side and steadied Lexi as she set her eyes on the closest hospital issued wheelchair. Lexi had her own wheelchair; it came as a standard issue accessory with a diagnosis like hers. But, she had opted to leave it in the car in hopes of forcing her body to walk off the pain in her abdomen. After covering ten feet of ground, she realized that her goal would need to be altered. She wouldn't be walking to the elevators and into the ICS unit today. She would have to be satisfied with walking to the first wheelchair and riding the rest of the way.

"Hey ladies!" the charge nurse said as they slowly made their way past the ICS double doors and towards the desk.

"Hi," Lexi said with a forced smile. She was grateful that she had been given the gift of keeping her composure when it came to physical pain. It made her uncomfortable to make others worry unnecessarily about her. Chemo had affected her hearing, but she wasn't completely deaf. She heard what the doctors said and knew the odds she had been given at diagnosis. She knew what she was up against. She also knew that she would be okay, even if the doctors didn't yet believe it.

"How are you?" Lexi said with great effort. The energy she had expounded on her walk across the parking lot was quickly catching up to her. The growing pain that was developing in her side was in desperate need of a heat pack. She adjusted slightly in her wheelchair. Emily must've sensed the tightening in Lexi's jaw—a sure sign she was holding pain in—and quickly asked what room they were in.

Once they had been directed to their blue-walled room, Emily assisted Lexi from the chair to the plastic bed. With excruciating effort, Lexi was able to find a tolerable position and with the help of a heat pack, found a way to get her pain manageable again. A different nurse entered the room and began to fill them in on what to expect for this hospital stay. Lexi felt as if she was so comfortable with this routine by now that she could be on the ICS welcome committee herself. She listened to what could have been a playback recording of what to expect from her last hospital stay and tried to ignore the fact that the stabbing in her abdomen was spreading from a throbbing ache to a sharp pain. She focused on her breathing as Emily arranged her pillows to offer her body more support. A second nurse came into the room to assist with the setup of the transplant chemo. Emily methodically unpacked their copious amounts of luggage as Lexi watched the bright red fluid drip from the IV into her veins. The desire to respond to Ricky's text did not stand a chance against Doxorubicin. There was a reason this chemo was called the Red Devil.

Lexi grew feebler over the coming days, her frailty more evident with every move she made and every ragged breath she drew in. An oxygen cannula was added to her entourage of medical equipment in hopes of giving her lungs the support that they too often required. The pale pallor of her face adopted a slight yellow hue. The hours she spent awake swapped places with the time spent sleeping. She shuffled through her mandated nightly routines, completing them in Emily's arms and yearning for the solace of the plastic hospital mattress. Once back in bed she would replace her heat packs, hold her side and continue to pray for time to pass her by. Days passed with Lexi waking only for small amounts of time, merely to express the discomfort she felt. Her abdomen resembled a water balloon that had slowly begun to fill over the last few days. Her growing malaise led Lexi to believe it would surely burst at any moment.

The muffled voices of what must've been her nurse, maybe a doctor, and Emily entered Lexi's semi-conscious psyche.

"The results from the imaging of her abdomen we did earlier today have come back," a voice said. The cocktail of chemo, pain, and exhaustion made it hard for Lexi to concentrate. She wanted to be involved in the conversation if it was important, wanted to be aware of what was going on with her body and what that meant for her future. But, for now, all she could do was focus on breathing and holding her distended abdomen. The monitors beeped indicating her heart rate was again too high. She could mask most signs of her physical pain, but her traitorous heart rate always gave her away. Someone silenced the alarm, and she heard only the slow whir of the chemo as it traveled through the IV tubing and into her veins.

"Her intestines have become twisted in several areas due to the scar tissue that has spread like spider webs throughout her abdomen. We can thank the invasiveness of her two previous surgeries for that."

There was a pause. There was always a pause when the doctors brought her news like this, as they fruitlessly searched for a way to make the bad news palatable. Finally, the voice just came out with it.

"She can't have surgery right now. You're aware of the risks associated with the chemo we're giving her." Lexi assumed Emily nodded because the voice continued. "Her blood counts will drop within the next twenty-four to forty-eight hours and she will have absolutely no immune system in a day or two. If she were even to develop the smallest infection from surgery, something minor, it will run rampant in her body. She will be under attack with no defenses and no reserves. She will go septic and be completely helpless." Lexi's eyelids were far too heavy to open. However, she did not need to see Emily's face to feel her fears. "We will place a tube to keep her stomach completely empty in hopes things will work themselves out." The voice finished by saying, "I'm going to contact the surgical team and send your imaging results to them as well, just to be on the safe side." The voice didn't sound very hopeful, Lexi thought.

Time eluded Lexi. Its passage came in the form of a nurse opening the solid wooden door to her room. Lexi's arm would then be lifted slightly as the rough fabric of the blood pressure cuff slid around it. The crinkle of the cuff would drown out the hum of the constant pumps that flowed into Lexi's body as it squeezed her arm. She found herself grateful for the momentary respite provided by the white noise of the bedside machine. The nurse muttered a quick but genuine apology about cold hands before Lexi felt the thin familiar paper measuring tape circling her growing abdomen. The measuring tape pulled taut and was then released. Emily said the measurement aloud. By the tone in her voice, Lexi knew that her belly had continued to slowly balloon outward. The nurse covered Lexi back up with the blanket. Emily readjusted the blanket out of habit. Lexi methodically repositioned her hand over her left side as the purl of the pump once again filled the room, and she drifted out of consciousness.

Time had passed, Lexi just wasn't sure how much. A new voice entered and must have looked at Lexi's composed features curiously. This voice was clearly that of a surgeon. It had the distinct bluntness of someone that tired of being the most intelligent person in the room. His position meant that he was wearing green scrubs and was probably not what most would call a "people person." Surgeons always had a way of getting to the point. There would be no long pauses here. Things were black and white in their world. They had to be. Lexi appreciated that about them. Even if what they had to say was hard to hear, you always knew you were getting the full story. Lexi allowed her eyes to stay closed, deciding the effort to open the heavy lids should be saved for a more meaningful task.

"They called me to come look at you, but you certainly don't look like you need to be rushed into surgery," the surgeon responded frankly. Emily did not respond but Lexi could feel a change in the energy of the room. The surgeon saw only a girl lying still in a hospital bed with her eyes closed. This was the problem. Emily saw the tightness in Lexi's jaw, even when she tried to sleep. Emily felt how Lexi gripped her hand intermittently throughout the long hours of the night because of the pain. She took in the circles under Lexi's eyes, and pallor of her skin that could not fully be attributed to transplant. Her daughter was not the type to scream out in pain but subconsciously she was crying out in agony. Lexi's countenance was a mere mask used to cope with the anguish she was experiencing.

The surgeon looked at the chart in his hands and read over the measurements that had been taken over the previous hours. "With every situation we have to look at the risk versus the benefit. There is no question that Lexi would need surgery if she were healthy enough, but she's not. She wasn't really healthy enough for this second transplant. She is actively receiving transplant chemo right now. The chemo is fatal if her body is not healthy enough to recover after the transplant. In a day or two, right when the risk of infection after surgery is the highest, her counts will drop, meaning that she will have absolutely no immune system. She would have no way to fight off an infection should her body develop one, even the smallest one. I'm not willing to take the risk of operating on her. I know she is feeling horrible but let's wait through the night and see what the doctor on the next shift thinks. Looking over her charts and what she has already endured, I don't think her body can handle another major surgery right now."

Emily watched him walk from the room believing he had washed his hands of the complicated situation. Emily allowed her head to fall forward as she folded her arms. She no longer prayed for Lexi to be pain free. She wanted this for her daughter more than anything, but Lexi had told her months ago that her life was not meant to be easy. Instead, Emily bowed her head and prayed that time would pass without Lexi being fully aware of it. A tear rolled silently down Emily's sleep-deprived cheek. If Lexi had to endure pain, Emily prayed that she would be spared the memory of the worst of it. Within ten minutes, the large wooden door opened once again, and the pained face of the surgeon entered the room.

"The timing couldn't be worse," he said bluntly. "To operate on her now is not something I'm wanting to do. Her counts will drop in the next day or two meaning that she will have absolutely no way to fight an infection. This is the worst-case scenario to be doing an operation like this." Emily nodded trying to be patient at hearing the same warnings that had already been given to her twice that day. Why couldn't she have déjà vu that involved manicures and massages instead of surgeons and sepsis?

"We have no choice," the surgeon said bluntly. "They are preparing the operating room now. Her latest imaging results just came back. She has to have surgery now. It cannot wait until morning." He exited the room matter-of-factly.

Nice pep talk, Lex thought. Her eyes remained closed as she breathed her next trial in and exhaled it out. At this point her body was too weak to even want to protest. The thought of surgical recovery was wretched. The thought of continuing to get worse was unbearable. A small groan involuntarily escaped her lips. Emily rose and came to Lexi's bedside reflexively. She adjusted the pillows under her daughter's head and swallowed hard in an effort to gather her ability to speak.

"Did you hear what the doctor said?" Emily asked, willing an air of calmness to mask her deep-seated fear.

Lexi tried to nod her head.

"What are your thoughts?" Emily asked, knowing full well that thoughts were all she could ask for. Choices were becoming fewer and fewer, a commodity that now must be rationed. Lexi cashed in the extra energy she'd been saving to open her blue eyes and give Emily a small smile in hopes she wouldn't worry too much.

Kris headed up to the hospital. He had no trouble finding a parking spot at this hour. The daytime visitors and regular appointment patients had long since cleared out and made room for the after-hours club. He walked through the double doors, greeted the security guard, who recognized him, and headed straight to the operating room, hating that he knew where it was. The daytime desks of the receptionists resembled a ghost town, the monitors asleep with the rest of the world. Emily met Kris in the hallway. He walked towards her with open arms. No words were spoken as they held one another tight, consoling each other without speaking a word. Hand in hand they headed back to where Lexi was waiting to be taken into the operating room. Unlike her other surgeries, there was no waiting for her turn in line, or being taken to a room to be visited by an anesthesiologist while nurses flitted in and out. Lexi's bed was in the open area by the nurses' station. Everyone that was in this area tonight was here specifically for her surgery.

"Hey, Dado," Lexi said hoarsely, her vocal chords dry from lack of use. Seeing her dad's blue eyes look back at her always filled Lexi with a sense of protection and love. Having him there brought a wave of peace to the troubled waters of her heart.

"Hey, Kid," Kris said with love as he bent forward and kissed her bald head.

Lexi sat quietly with her parents outside of the operating room waiting for her third major surgery in just four months. The hum of the fluid running through her veins seemed to echo in the quiet halls. Kris looked helplessly at the face of the child he had watched grow into a beautiful young woman. He would do anything to take this trial from her. Anything.

The surgeon approached Lexi's bedside and reiterated the procedure that she would endure and then exhaled before discussing with Kris and Emily the risks involved, once again. Her parents each held one of Lexi's hands in theirs as they listened to the words that were spoken. Lexi hated this part. She hated the worry that was so clearly painted on her parents' faces. She had been told what would need to be done for her to conquer the mountain before her. She didn't need continual reminders of all the likely boulders that lay strewn about her path. She wanted only to begin her ascent. Lexi felt Kris softly kiss the top of her once again bald head as Emily whispered, "I love you," in a soft voice that was strong with emotion.

Lexi offered a feeble squeeze of each of their hands. In her mind she also smiled at them, but she wasn't sure if she had the physical energy to materialize the gesture from her thoughts into action. The hospital bed began rolling towards the operating room and away from Kris and Emily. Lexi tightened her grip on her abdomen as the nurse navigating the bed slowly turned from the hall into the familiar room. The nurse spoke calmly, and the anesthesiologist added an IV to the collection of tubes going into Lexi's body. Under the direction of the anesthesiologist, the nurse began to count backwards from ten. 10, 9, 8, 7, 6 . . .

Emily's phone buzzed in her hand. She exhaled into the sanitized air of the four blue walls before looking to see who it was. The events of last night's surgery still played on repeat in her mind. The surgeon had found Emily and Kris in the empty waiting room and reported that things were far more concerning than the imaging had originally led him to believe. Nonetheless, he was able to leave Lexi's body in the best possible condition he could, given the circumstances. He echoed his concerns and told Kris and Emily to pray for an uneventful few days. Emily blew out her breath and felt the exhaustion evident in the deep ache of her bones. The phone buzzed again, bringing her back to the present.

"Hey, Sister Gould! How's my friend Lexi doing? I texted her a few days ago and she hasn't texted me back. It usually takes her longer to respond when she's in the hospital, but it's been longer than normal. Is everything okay? Do you guys need anything?"

A warmth touched Emily's heart. Ricky's cancer path may not have mirrored Lexi's, but he had traveled a similar road. His understanding reached beyond his years and bore witness of the miles he'd journeyed. Regardless, he was still a teenage boy who had his own life to worry about. Emily looked at the blue walls surrounding her and then to Lexi who lay resting in her bed, still chained to her IV pole. The yellowing of Lexi's skin had begun to give way to the pale pallor that accompanied transplant. The dull whir of the last dose of chemo provided enough white noise to drown out any thoughts of what tomorrow might bring. Emily decided to spare Ricky the full reality of Lexi's current situation and opt for a lighter version of the truth.

"Yeah, she's doing okay. She had to have surgery yesterday. Everything went well and she's just recovering. I'm not sure if she has the strength to hold her phone yet, haha." She set the phone back in her lap and leaned her head against the small couch that doubled as her bed. The faint smell of bleach touched her senses and her phone buzzed again.

Rather than calming Ricky's nerves, Emily's words seemed to have stirred them.

"I was just thinking of coming up there and hanging out with you guys for a little bit tonight if that's okay. I don't want to bug you, but if y'all wouldn't mind the company, I'd like to come see Lex."

Emily took a deep breath. Lexi would never pass on the chance to hang out with Ricky. But tonight would greatly differ from their usual hangouts. Ricky deserved a clearer picture of the portrait Lexi was living in these days, not the snapshot Emily had offered him. Emily thought for a moment and then responded.

"You know that you are always welcome to come and hang out, but Lex is really weak these days. Her body is struggling pretty bad right now. It takes too much energy for her to stay awake for long periods of time. She always loves to see you, but I'm not really sure that she'll be up to playing a game or even talking much tonight."

Mere seconds passed before Emily's phone buzzed. "Okay, I'll see you guys after practice. Tell Lex it's okay if she just sleeps. I get that she needs her rest. I just want to see her and make sure she's doing okay. Thanks, Sister Gould!"

Ricky strolled through the double doors and effortlessly hiked up the four flights of stairs to the cancer unit. The nurses outside of Lexi's room greeted him warmly.

"How's my friend today?" he asked as he approached the desk they were sitting at. There was no need to clarify who he was talking about; he had become one of the hospital regulars whenever Lexi was inpatient.

"She's a rock star," her nurse replied with a soft smile. Her hand rested on a large binder with Lexi's name on it that she had been charting in.

"I know that, but is she feeling any better?" Ricky said, hoping for more insight on Lexi's condition.

"It's been a rough few days," the nurse said plainly. Her kind eyes held equal amounts of love and pain; sorrow and hope. One could only imagine the depths her heart held. "It seems like our girl is hitting every bump in the road," the nurse replied solemnly. She smiled at Ricky kindly and returned to her binder once again.

Ricky walked to Lexi's door and exhaled with purpose, knowing he needed to gather himself before opening the door. Lexi had enough to worry about without him adding his fears to the pile. The shade on the heavy wooden door was drawn. A child's drawings played on the window complete with butterflies, rainbows, flowers, and misshapen hearts in a variety of sizes. Due to hospital protocol, patients were not allowed to enter one another's room. But, that did not stop them from finding ways to connect with each other and spread joy. Lexi had told Ricky of a friend whom she had made a poster for and then asked a nurse to hang it on his door to brighten his day. Another time she had decorated a small girl's door with hearts to bring a smile to her face. Today it looked as if one of Lexi's little friends had come to return the favor by lifting her spirits with their artwork.

Seeing the brightly colored masterpiece on the door caused the tension in Ricky's chest to loosen slightly and he knocked on the door. He heard Emily's voice call for him to come in. He slowly opened the door to a dimly lit room. The blue walls that were meant to offer serenity reflected the sky at dusk. Lexi looked to be uncomfortably asleep in her hospital bed. *Did anyone ever really sleep comfortably in the hospital?* Ricky thought. He recalled the many nights that his 6'2" frame had unsuccessfully tried to fold into a bed designed for someone half his size. Eventually, he resorted to removing the footboard off of the bed and allowing his feet to dangle liberally like a small child at the edge of a pool.

Emily stood to greet him as he entered the room, but Lexi didn't stir. His entrance caused no reaction from her. He forced a smile and hoped it looked genuine enough that his concern wasn't evident in his eyes.

"Hey," he said to Emily as he walked over and gave her a quick hug. "How's my friend doing tonight?" He turned to look at Lexi lying in the bed. The tubing ran from the IV pole to her veins with the same smooth rhythm it had run through his. A small cannula delivered oxygen to her petite nose in little puffs every few moments, and the red light on her pointer finger indicated that, for now, it was doing its job.

Ricky grabbed a stool and sat beside the bed, feeling the need to just be close to Lexi. He looked from Lexi to Emily, waiting for a response. He saw Emily take a deliberate breath in and he knew she was working on choosing her words carefully.

"She's doing okay, just resting."

"She's really pretty out of it tonight," he said, unable to keep the worry from seeping into his voice. Emily nodded slightly and quickly changed the subject.

"So, are you planning on leaving for your mission right after high school?" she asked.

The misdirect was not lost on Ricky but it seemed as if they could all use the opportunity to escape the cloudy blue walls, if only through conversation.

"Actually, I'm going to try to graduate early," Ricky answered. "My plan is to graduate right after the third quarter so that I can leave on my mission and get back. That will give me a chance to start playing basketball sooner."

"Wow! That's impressive. It's hard to catch up in school after having cancer, so to be able to graduate early is pretty cool," Emily responded enthusiastically. "If you could pick, where would you want to go on your mission?"

"Germany," Ricky said assuredly.

"You sound pretty confident in that," Emily replied with a smile.

"Well, I was born there so I have dual citizenship. I'm fluent in the language so it makes sense," Ricky explained. "I know you can't pick where you serve, but I am pretty sure that is where I will be going."

"Will they send you out of the country after a cancer diagnosis?" asked Emily. "I've heard a few people have had some struggles with their papers after treatment. Have you been cancer free long enough?"

"I think I'll be okay. They have good medical care over there and my parents still know a few people. So, if anything did happen, I would be really well taken care of. But, I'm not worried. By the time I go out I will have been cancer free for over three years. I haven't even had a scare or any sign of relapse since being done with treatment. I think my cancer days are behind me."

"I sure hope so," Emily said. "Having cancer once is horrible. No one should ever have to face it twice in their lives," she added.

"My mom said that the timing for my cancer was perfect," Ricky said. He noticed the quizzical look on Emily's face and continued on. "Staffords aren't known for their humility, and I had an extra dose of confidence because I was good at basketball and got tall so fast. Cancer was exactly what I needed to learn a bit of humility. I've learned my lesson though, so I don't think I'll have to go through it again." A low moan interrupted their conversation.

Lex softly groaned again. The conversation instantly fell to the ground like the house of cards it was. Emily immediately went to her bedside. Ricky stood to see how he could be of assistance. Emily leaned in close to hear what Lexi was saying and then looked at Ricky and spoke.

"I just need to help her sit up for a minute and then help her walk to the restroom," Emily said. Her tone was slightly apologetic, but resolved to the knowledge that this was their lot for now.

Ricky didn't move immediately. Instead, he watched Emily place her hands under Lexi's small frame and then mirrored her actions in an attempt to help gently lift Lexi's torso up. Lexi's face grimaced in pain and the heart rate monitors responded in suit, showing the escalation as a result of the pain that the movement brought on. Emily worked efficiently to remove the cannula and oximeter, while simultaneously directing Ricky which buttons to touch on the bedside monitor to silence the beeping noises.

"Can you move your legs off of the bed yourself?" Emily asked Lexi.

Ricky saw Lexi's jaw tighten as her eyes remained shut. She nodded ever so slightly. Ricky gently placed his hands on her back to help steady her. He carefully watched as Lexi willed each of her legs to move from off the bed and onto the floor. Her eyes closed tight and her brows furrowed with a fusion of determination and suffering. He had never witnessed such strength firsthand. It was heroic. She took a moment to regain her strength and, with help, was finally able to shakily stand. He moved her IV pole around the bed and into one of Emily's waiting hands. Lexi grasped Emily's elbows for support. Her bald head hung forward and Ricky could see the top of her shoulder blades protruding from her hospital gown. She had undoubtedly lost more weight. Ricky watched momentarily as she inched slowly towards her destination with the steadying hand of her mom. He quietly opened the heavy door, stepped out of the room with the four blue walls, and waited until he could be back at her side.

Ricky had been through cancer, he had gone through chemo, and it was horrible. It was beyond horrible. But this was something else. Over the last few days Lex had taken longer and longer to message him back. He had become concerned, he didn't know exactly why, just that something didn't feel right. When he asked if she was okay, she simply responded, "I will be, my body is just struggling a little bit right now." She then turned the conversation to him and what he was doing.

Pfff. A little bit, he thought to himself. Lexi had gone through her second transplant in less than as many months. She had just had surgery. She couldn't even sit up on her own, let alone walk. No wonder he hadn't heard much from her. Her phone was probably too heavy for her feeble hands to hold. She probably told Emily how to respond to his last few texts and then Emily typed them out for her to send to him. How could she be going through this and say that she was struggling *a little bit?*

Ricky took a walk down the familiar hospital hall to the ice machine. Maybe Lexi would be up for some ice chips when she made it back to her bed. His feet made progress forward, but his mind kept spinning on the hamster wheel it had boarded as soon as he entered Lexi's room. He reeled at seeing Lexi in the state she was in. He breathed out audibly trying to process what was happening. As he did, the recollection of a conversation he and Lexi had replayed in his mind.

Lexi had told him that when she was first diagnosed, she was promised in a priesthood blessing that this was not the end of her life, but the beginning. A nagging voice reminded Ricky that he had been at the hospital enough to overhear the doctors and nurses talking too. They didn't always share Lexi's optimism. The voice attacked again with the knowledge that she was unequivocally frailer during his last few interactions with her. Lexi had just brushed it off to being tired or having a rough day. Something had told Ricky it was more than that, and he knew that Lexi was trying to protect him from it.

Ricky knew that he couldn't go back into Lexi's room with sadness in his eyes. Lexi rarely showed weakness and she strongly disliked feeling as if people came to visit just to pity her. She did not feel bad for herself or the situation she was in, and she would not allow others to feel bad for her either. She knew she would survive, regardless of what she would endure. Despite the unsurety of her future, Ricky did not want her to have to endure it alone.

Ricky returned from his walk with water for himself and Emily, ice chips for Lexi, and a determination that he would hold to his faith in God and the promises that were made to Lexi. Emily opened the door and Ricky entered the room. The shade on the window to the outside world was open, allowing a soft light to graze the room. The walls resembled the blue of the sky after a thunderstorm. Lexi was composed in her bed, surrounded by an army of pillows that were supporting her body like soldiers protecting their war-torn captain. Her IV pole had returned to its post next to her bedside, and her monitors were reattached and reading well. Her heart rate was still escalated from the exertion of the small walk. Ricky couldn't help but notice that Lexi was sitting very still focusing on her breathing. The cannula in her small nose was securely in place. Her blue eyes were open, and she greeted him with a weak but genuine smile that caused his heart to fill with gratitude.

"Hey," Ricky said. "Look who's awake."

"Hey," Lex responded. "How long have you been here?"

"Not too long," he responded. If Lexi didn't remember him being there when she needed help to stand, he didn't want to bring it up. She wasn't one that liked to show other people her struggles. He knew it wasn't a matter of pride but a matter of making sure that she was not the cause of someone else's worry. "How are you doing?" Ricky asked.

"I'm okay, how are you? Are you getting excited for your upcoming tournament?" He smiled at her authentic response. Here she was unable to walk on her own and Lexi genuinely wanted to know how his life was going. She kept still, something Ricky may not have noticed much without being there for the preamble of their visit. He wondered how many times she had spent her days in darkness and then composed herself in time for a visit. He never would have been the wiser. After ten short minutes, her eyelids had grown far too heavy and, despite her desire to spend more time with him, Lexi could no longer hold the conversation. She drifted off to sleep and Ricky turned to Emily.

"Why is she struggling so much with this transplant?" he asked pointedly. There would be no changing the subject this time. He needed more information.

"Well, within the last four months she has had three major abdominal surgeries and two transplants. This was after she received the most toxic chemo that they use to treat childhood cancer. To be honest, her body wasn't healthy enough for any of this. The treatment is taking its toll on her."

He was silent for a minute and then responded. "But she'll be okay. She told me that she'll be okay." He meant it as a statement but couldn't help the question from seeping through. After seeing her tonight and knowing that there was still so much treatment that Lexi needed to go through, his mind needed some kind of verbal affirmation.

"That's what she tells me too," Emily said with a melancholy smile.

Ricky looked at Lexi's frame lying in the bed a moment longer. He thought of the battle she was facing, not just the physical one but the mental one. He thought how much she had lost and how hard she was working to get it all back. He thought of how far she had come, and how far she still had to go.

"I'll be so happy for her when she can dance again," Ricky said while looking at the monitor that showed Lexi's heart rate had finally returned to normal.

"Me too." Emily said wistfully.

Chapter 5

"Think how joyous each and every day could be when you are making the most of what you have." —Chrissy Halton

It was the last week of June and Lexi had officially engrafted for the second time in her almost 16 years of life. Healing slowly took place in her feeble frame. Her body reconstructed itself cell by cell and she felt the pull of her muscles as they learned to work once more. With determination she pushed her bones to complete the mundane tasks that she used to take for granted. With each session of physical therapy, Lexi pushed herself beyond exhaustion. Her body responded in kind by shaking indefinitely. She learned to control the small tremors by clenching her jaw tightly in place until the quaking had subsided. The muscles surrounding her mandible ached in protest, but it was preferable to the pain that came from the uncontrollable rattling of her teeth. Today was a good day. She was able to, once again, walk unassisted.

The fourth of July was soon approaching. Lexi should be preparing to march down Main Street in the hometown parade that her community put on each year. Her long, brown hair should be slicked back and her eyelids should be painted with gold glitter. Fake eyelashes and red lipstick should be the finishing touch to ensure that Lexi looked just like every other girl on her drill team. Her friends and family should have to search to find her among the body of blue sparkled costumes, the precise combination of their appearance and movement molding the girls into perfect unison as they executed each parade command.

After the sun had begun its retirement on America's day her family should be joining together in a barbecue with Kris manning the grill. Granny should bring the pork and beans that Lexi never understood why anyone ate. The night should finish off with her family seated on denim blankets made from the jeans that she and her siblings had outgrown. They should be surrounded by their closest friends at the park by her house. They should all be watching the sky wide eyed and open mouthed as the small-town committee put on a big town display of freedom.

But Lexi learned months ago that the life she thought she should be living was not the life she had been given. She closed her eyes and allowed her mind to be transported to her "should be" life for just a moment. Just then, there was a knock. A nurse entered the room to take Lexi's vitals, and her "should be" life escaped through the open door. She watched it go, knowing she did not have the energy to chase after it today. Lexi breathed as deeply as her lungs would allow and looked around at her reality. She was still in her small hospital room surrounded by four blue walls that were covered with drawings and homemade cards from her little sisters and friends that had come to visit. Cam had written her a note on the white board that ran the length of the cupboard that held all of her personal belongings. Ricky had sequestered the top part of that same board on his last visit to draw her a stick figure picture of himself with a basketball, complete with the spiky hair. Everyone had done their best to make the room feel more like home, but "like home" wasn't home and Lexi was missing it today more than ever.

Another knock sounded on the door and Emily rose to answer it. Lexi heard the quiet voice of a woman that she didn't recognize. Emily stepped into the hall, closing the heavy wooden door behind her. Lexi had only moments to wonder who the new visitor might be before Emily re-entered the room with a grin.

"There is a mom out there with her son. They have been inpatient for awhile and are finally on their way home. Her son heard that you like it when people play the ukulele and sing to you. He was wondering if he could come sing you a song before he goes home."

Lexi's face answered before her words could. Her eyes lit up and she could hardly contain the overwhelming warmth that filled her soul at the realization that someone who had broken free of their hospital room had thought to make a stop to sing to her on their way out. Emily smiled brightly as she held open the door to reveal a young man, once again with a full head of hair. The boy, who couldn't have been more than 11, shyly smiled with a brief wave of his hand as his mom told Lexi that his name was Tanner. Lexi smiled warmly and introduced herself. He hurried on before the courage he'd worked up escaped his 5'5" frame.

"I heard you liked to listen to people sing, and I like to play the ukulele so I thought I'd come sing you a song before I leave the hospital."

Lexi beamed her encouragement, which was all the approval Tanner needed.

> *You are my sunshine, my only sunshine.*
> *You make me happy when skies are gray.*
> *You'll never know, dear, how much I love you.*
> *Please don't take my sunshine away.*

Lexi's heart filled with love beyond capacity to hold it. She looked at the boy before her, his bright red hair dancing like a flame that had tried to unsuccessfully be tamed atop his head. His rounded cheeks, a distinct characteristic of the prednisone he was likely taking to offset the side effects of his treatment, were flush against his pale skin. She found herself drawn to the depth of his young eyes and the wealth of knowledge they held. It was as if the honest love he carried for others was as plain to her as the freckles on his face. Her smile deepened as he asked if she would like to hear another song. She didn't hesitate and neither did he as he began with a Disney favorite. The impromptu concert ended after the second ballad as both musician and audience had exhausted their energies but given life to a new friendship.

Lexi said goodbye to Tanner and his mom, Megan, then she laid her head back on her pillow and prayed that sleep would find her heavy lids long before memories of the traditions of years past broke through her foggy consciousness to torment her once again.

Emily placed one hand on the heavy wooden door as her other hand pushed the door handle in an effort to keep it from making unnecessary noise. Her efforts were in vain. Lexi could feel the presence of her mom and sleepily opened her eyes. Emily wore her emotions on her sleeve, she couldn't help it. She had come hardwired that way. She was the type of person you wanted to tell all your secrets to, but none of your surprises. The look on her face said that something exciting lay in store. Today was going to be a good day.

"What's going on?" Lexi said, trying to match the enthusiasm on Emily's face. Emily looked at her with a mischievous grin as she sat easily on the end of Lexi's bed.

"Do you know what day it is?"

"Thursday?" Lexi answered.

"Actually it's Monday, but it's also the Fourth of July!" Emily replied. "But that's not the best part." Emily looked as if she might burst if she couldn't share her surprise soon. "I just got permission to sneak you out of your room tonight to go watch fireworks on the bridge at the end of the hall!" Emily said, the elation evident in her eyes.

"Really?" Lexi said in disbelief. She hadn't been out of her room in over three weeks. She had not even been cleared to leave the room for walks on the ICS unit, let alone walks on the fourth floor.

"Yep!" Emily said, clearly proud of the surprise that was reflected in Lexi's eyes. "I will just push your wheelchair down there and as long as you are good to wear your mask, we can watch the fireworks from a big window tonight!"

Lexi felt a sudden rush of emotions. Against all odds, she would be granted this one freedom, this one liberty, this one link to her past life. Not only would she get to see fireworks tonight, she would get the chance to leave the ICS unit to see them! The thought nearly brought tears to her eyes.

Nighttime came and the clinic quieted. Although the different medications made it so that a typical sleeping schedule was out of the question for most patients, the majority of residents stayed in their rooms during the evening hours. Around 9:30 p.m Lexi and Emily began their preparations to momentarily leave the azure walls. By 9:45

they left the four blue walls behind. Just outside of the double doors and down the hall, they found themselves heading back to a piece of a world Lexi thought had been abandoned.

Emily parked the wheelchair and, after making sure Lexi was comfortable, pulled out her phone. Lexi tried to peer over, only to be caught.

"Hey, eyes on your own paper, chief!" Emily said jokingly.

Lexi laughed and looked out the window waiting anxiously for the show to start. Just then she noticed on her left a few bright colors in the distance lighting up the sky. Their brilliance reminded Lexi of the sparklers she used to hold in her hands as a child.

"Look there!" Emily said as she pointed to the right. Another fireworks show had started simultaneously. Seemingly out of nowhere "God Bless America" started to play and Lexi looked to Emily who shrugged and held up her phone.

"I wanted it to be like a real firework show so I YouTubed patriotic songs," she said simply. "Happy Fourth of July, honey."

"This is definitely a firework show that I will never forget," Lexi said as she watched show after show compete with one another behind the thick hospital glass. "Happy Fourth of July, Momma."

The following days, Lexi's heart spurred her body into action once again. Her blood counts responded in kind and, after being inpatient for just over a month, she was finally well enough to leave the hospital once more. Six rounds of chemo, check. Three major surgeries, check. Two transplants in two months, check. *Bring on the radiation*, she thought to herself.

Chapter 6

"The ability to wait is the sign of true love. Be patient
and you'll get everything you want."
—Kamlesh Makholiyah

A month had passed since Lexi had broken free of her IV pole and
four blue walls. She had transitioned from transplant to radiation. To her surprise, radiation had offered a much needed respite for
her tattered body. But today, Lexi wasn't thinking about treatment.
Today, Lexi was officially sixteen.

Ricky wasn't sure exactly what that meant for them or exactly why
he was so excited. But one thing was certain—he could now officially
ask Lexi on a date. This thought caused his emotions to blend together
into the perfect sundae of nervousness and excitement with a cherry
of hope on top.

It had been five months since Ricky was first introduced to Lexi.
Five months of hanging out at the hospital and texting regularly
whenever she was up to it. From the moment he saw her, something
inside of Ricky said that Lexi was special, but he tried to write it off
to the fact that he was just drawn to the life he had once been forced
to live. However, the more time he spent with Lexi the more he knew
this wasn't the case. She was the kind of girl you didn't get sick of,
the kind you could spend all day with and still want to talk to while
driving home. Lexi was the kind of girl who didn't demand perfec-
tion from you but somehow knew you were capable of great things.
She was the kind that challenged him. Lexi easily broke through the

surface of Ricky that he had constructed to impress others. She saw him, the him he kept hidden. When he was around her, everything was right in Ricky's world.

Ricky wasn't sure when he had accepted the fact that he looked at Lexi as more than a friend. He couldn't pinpoint an exact moment in time that his feelings for her had changed; it was more of a collection of several small moments. It just seemed like the natural course that one would take with Lexi. You meet her. You get to know her. You fall in love with her. The End. Looking back, he supposed it was inevitable. There was no use fighting it anymore, so why try? He made up his mind then and there. Tonight, at her birthday party, he was going to tell Lexi how he felt about her. Then he was going to kiss her.

He didn't have time to get all the details ironed out. He hadn't thought about where or when he would do it. He figured he would play it by ear and wait until the moment was absolutely magical. Through roundabout conversations, and a bit of recon on his part, Ricky had learned that Lexi hadn't had her first kiss yet and he wanted the moment to be absolutely perfect for her. He had been paying extra attention to their conversations lately and although Lexi kept things pretty low key, he was fairly confident she had the same feelings for him that he was having for her. If that were the case, then tonight would mean a big change in their relationship—as long as he didn't chicken out.

For the entire forty-five-minute drive he hyped himself up and knew that this was meant to be. This is where things were going. He was Ricky Stafford and tonight, on her sixteenth birthday, he would be Alexis Gould's first kiss. He exited the freeway and began to follow the directions on his phone to the address Lex had given him. He came to the red light and stopped. As he glanced to his left, he noticed the truck next to him. Although the original color of the truck was blue, rust spots were fighting to take over. The enviro-enemy vehicle sported an American flag and had a live goat with one horn riding in the back. Ricky looked over at the goat slowly and it peered at him as if he was clearly the one out of place. Lex had told him that Magna still had that small town feel to it. She wasn't kidding. He laughed to himself and refocused. Tonight he had to be on top of his game. If he wanted to kiss Lexi, he couldn't waste time getting distracted by the unicorn of Magna. Lex wasn't just some girl you decided to kiss and then it happened. He needed a plan.

Ricky continued down the street and then took a left and another left into the parking lot of what looked to be a small, family-owned Mexican restaurant. *Cool place for a party*, he thought. *Except no one else is here.* There must have been some mistake. He did not drive all by himself for almost an hour just to spend the whole night hanging out alone. Lexi had told him he was welcome to bring some friends, even suggesting that he could meet some of her friends and she could meet some of his. Right now, that felt more like competition and less like a good idea. He was grateful he had chosen not to invite anyone else.

Ricky pulled out his phone to text Lexi for clarification on the address. He quickly realized that the party had already started and she likely wouldn't be staring at her phone. Instead, he called Emily to ask for directions and quickly found his way to a neighborhood not far from the small Mexican restaurant. He pulled up to the house where the party was at and a small rush of adrenaline quickly surged through his veins. He took a deep breath and exited the car.

There was music coming from the backyard and he easily found a sidewalk lined with flower beds that wound around the house. It led him to a spacious backyard with a long, grassy area. A few tables had been arranged on the patio close to the house where the BBQ was. He noticed that Kris and Emily were hovering over these tables making sure that all of the food was fully stocked. Along the side of the yard were several other tables, set up with chairs for people to sit at and eat or just visit. Towards the back of the yard, he noticed a sand volleyball pit and smiled. He could easily take up residence there all night if need be.

He greeted Emily and she introduced him to Kris, although the introduction wasn't necessary. One glance at Kris and it was evident that he was Lexi's dad.

"Hey, Ricky," Kris said as he looked him in the eyes. He had the same blue eyes that Lexi did, but in his face they made Ricky nervous for a whole different reason. Lexi adored Kris and often spoke to Ricky about the special relationship she and her dad shared. Likewise, she had told Kris all about Ricky and how he had recently become such an important part of her life.

"Hey, Brother Gould," Ricky said, shaking Kris's hand firmly. Kris made a face as if he had just tasted something sour.

"Usually people just call me Kris, or Coach." He said bluntly. "You don't need to worry about the 'Brother Gould' stuff," he added while still looking at Ricky. Kris then broke into half grin which Ricky promptly returned, both out of habit and nervousness.

"Lex is around here somewhere," Emily said. "She will be excited that you made it." Ricky's heart involuntarily quickened at the thought of seeing Lex. He wondered how long his heart had known he was falling for Lexi before his head caught up to the realization. Whatever the case, it was nice to have them both on board now. He quickly scanned the small congregations of teens and found her. Lexi's bald head was gleaming in the sunlight, a contrast to the hair-covered scalps surrounding her. However, Ricky had come to know enough about Lexi that— bald head or not—she would've stuck out in any crowd. She wasn't designed to fit in.

Lexi was encircled by a few of her friends, most likely from school. Ricky had never seen her in this type of setting before. She was not shackled down to an IV pole, and there was currently no medication coursing through her veins. The blue walls had given way to an endless blue sky that knew no bounds. Lexi wore white shorts, a light-colored tee, and had a jacket tied around her petite waist.

Ricky took note that Lexi took time to greet everyone who came to the party as if they were the most important guest. It may have been her party, but she did her best to make certain that she was not the center of attention. To Lexi, everyone was important. It didn't matter if you had hair or no hair, could dunk a basketball or needed a wheelchair to get around, Lexi had a way of letting you know that you were genuinely loved and that you mattered. Whether she was in the hospital or at a backyard birthday party, Lexi was constant. She was consistently taking time to get to know people and let them know what they meant to her individually. This trait alone set her apart. She didn't have to try to impress others. They were drawn to her because of the tangible way they felt love from her. Perhaps Ricky was drawn to her for the same reason.

Ricky exhaled with purpose and reminded himself that he didn't drive all this way to admire Lexi from afar. He strolled across the grass and caught her attention. He couldn't help but notice how her eyes seemed to light up a little more when they looked at him—at least he hoped they did and that it wasn't just wishful thinking. He hugged her tightly and held on a little longer than he should have. They talked for a few minutes before other friends arrived and volleyed for Lexi's attention.

Ricky stepped away and Lexi looked at him quizzically.

"You're hanging out for awhile, right?" she called as he was backing up from the small circle of friends that was forming.

"Yeah, I'm planning on staying all night. I'm going to go see what's going on over there," Ricky said as he motioned towards the sand volleyball pit. "Come find me in a bit when you get a break from your fan club," he added teasingly. Lexi rolled her eyes mockingly and agreed as she turned back to her small group of friends.

Ricky quickly found himself down by the volleyball net with a few of the other party goers. Some of them seemed to recognize him from the pictures Lexi had posted on Instagram of the first time he came up to visit her. A few of them even knew his name. He hoped that meant that Lexi talked about him to her friends. He made his way into the rotation of the volleyball game and began to find his groove on the court. He had always been athletic by nature, and growing up in a family full of competitors, he found himself feeling right at home. However, he didn't want to showcase all of his athleticism as it might seem a little off putting to people that were just there to have a good time. That being said, he was determined to showcase enough to impress Lex, who he was hoping would make her way over to watch a few games. Ricky took his turn serving the volleyball and then rotated through each of the positions. He made it back to where he started and rotated out as the next person rotated in.

"Hey, Ricky!" one of Lexi's friends said as she came walking over with another girl. Ricky was standing on the sidelines, and it would be a few minutes before it was his turn to go back in.

"Hey," Ricky said to the girls, feeling bad he didn't know their names. They didn't seem to notice his lack of familiarity, and they continued on with their agenda as planned.

"So, Lex said you're from Orem?" the first girl asked with a slight raise in her brow.

"Yep," Ricky said with a smile, not entirely sure where this was going. He had heard that everyone in Magna was fiercely loyal to their local high school, and he wasn't sure if things were about to get awkward.

"That's cool," said the second girl. Ricky couldn't help but notice that both of them could scarcely contain their smiles and he was pretty certain it had very little to do with where he attended high school. He just smiled and nodded.

"Yep," he said as he waited to see if they were planning on continuing the conversation.

"That's a long way to come just for a friend's birthday party," hinted the first girl.

"Well, Lexi is not just a friend, she's my best friend. And it's worth the drive to hang out with her," Ricky replied.

Bingo. That's what the giggling girls had been looking for. Suddenly all bets were off. Simultaneously their faces split into wide grins as they nudged one another and tried to stifle their giggles.

"Do you like her?" asked the first girl with a hopeful smile on her face.

Ricky figured that there was no use trying to fight it any longer—maybe Giggles McGee and her friend might prove to even be some pretty helpful wingmen if it came down to it. Ricky honestly didn't know who they were or what their relationship with Lexi was like, but he figured he could use all the help he could get tonight.

"Yeah," he said with a smile. "I've got a pretty big crush on my best friend."

Someone from the court called his name and he realized that it was his turn to rotate back into the game. Thankful for the distraction, he began to stroll away and prayed the buzzing in his veins wasn't visible to anyone else.

"Just so you know, she likes you too," the second girl said in the loudest whisper Ricky had ever heard. A rush of exhilaration went through his body like a welcome jolt of energy that began in his core and flowed freely through his limbs. He could tell that he was smiling like a little kid who had found a secret piece of candy in his pocket, but he didn't care. This new revelation left him pulled between wanting to stand on a chair to shout his feelings for Lexi or keep them hidden just a little longer, knowing they were too precious to expose so carelessly. For now, he just found himself somewhat relieved. He wasn't sure if it was due to the unloading of emotions he'd been carrying or that he was no longer being interrogated. Either way, he sauntered on to the court with confidence in much more than just his volleyball game.

Before long, Lexi made her way over to the volleyball pit. She found a spot on a blanket that had been laid out in the grass. A few of her friends had gathered to watch the ongoing volleyball game and she casually joined them. She tried to take in the game as a whole but it was no use. Without effort, Ricky Stafford seemed to capture her attention, yet again, but it had nothing to do with his physical abilities. She noticed how easily Ricky got along with everyone else, even people who were different from him. She noticed how he took time getting to know people that didn't seem to know anyone else.

People's feelings had always been important to Lexi. As she watched Ricky's interactions with people he had never met, Lexi realized that they seemed to be important to him as well. The thought made her lips turn upward into an unconscious smile as her heart quickened.

Not many people could make the transition from the heavy emotions that often accompanied hospital life to laughing and joking at a backyard barbecue. Yet, here she sat watching Ricky do just that. This same boy that would sit for hours keeping her company amidst the four blue walls was now playing volleyball with her friends and family under the open blue sky at her birthday party, and somehow it felt as natural as the first time she put on ballet slippers.

Ricky was so comfortable in his own skin that he drove all this way by himself just to come hang out at her birthday party. She watched as he effortlessly laughed and joked with those around him. She noted that every time he did something funny, he stole a glance her way to see if she noticed. Their eyes would lock quickly before Ricky would be reminded by his teammates that it was his turn to serve or that he needed to rotate. Lexi enjoyed watching him play. She was excited for him to be healthy enough to begin doing the things he liked to do once again. He had told her about some of the basketball tournaments he had played in this past summer and the success he had seen. He continued to amaze her. Not even cancer could keep Ricky Stafford from accomplishing his dreams.

Lexi found herself thinking of all of the things Ricky could do in his life. Sure, he could play basketball—that was a given. Although she had never actually seen him in a game, she could see the passion in his eyes when he talked about it and was sure that he must be good. But there was so much more to him than that. Anyone could learn to play a sport, or work hard and become an athlete. Just as easily, anyone could lose that ability. But Ricky was more than his physical abilities. He was so much deeper than the young man that had projected surface confidence the first time that they had met in clinic. Over the past few months, conversations had revealed a version of Ricky that he seemed to keep hidden from the world. He let his guard down and allowed himself to be vulnerable. The Ricky that she knew was kind and caring. He wasn't motivated by worldly praise or driven by pride. His confidence gave way to consideration. He esteemed connection over attention. He wasn't concerned with what other people thought. He valued God above all else. She hoped that one day he would see himself the way that she saw him.

Ricky noticed a group of guys that looked to be his same age. They casually walked across the lawn towards Lexi carrying a bouquet of balloons. Ricky's heart stumbled. Of course he wasn't the only one aware that Lexi turning sixteen meant that she would start dating. He recognized some of the guys from playing against them in basketball tournaments. Ricky took a minute to take in the scene before him and assess the competition. The guys assembled like a typical basketball team. The stout point guard stood out front leading the way. The shooting guard and small forward looked as if their gangly limbs were almost too long for their thin frames. They flanked their point guard out of habit on either side. The power forward and center filled in the ensemble, standing a few inches taller than their friends. The group seemed nice enough and by the way Lexi laughed and smiled at them. She was clearly comfortable around them. A few moments passed and then Lexi hugged them one by one.

Ricky found himself wishing his makeshift volleyball team was on the opposite side of the sand court. This would give him a better vantage point to possibly hear what was being said. The boys stayed and talked a little longer. He found himself trying to decide if Lexi was being nice or if she was into the conversation. What if one of them was already asking her out? What if he was over here like a chump playing volleyball and making lame jokes with people he had just met while someone else was swooping in on his best friend?

Lexi glimpsed his way and Ricky realized she'd caught him staring. He smiled quickly and she returned the motion before returning to chat with her friends.

Wow, she is beautiful, he thought. Her lashes had come and gone since he had known her, and she was excited that they had recently just started coming back again. She had begun to put weight back on and he couldn't help but notice her long, athletic legs. Years of dancing had paid off. She looked completely comfortable surrounded by the group of people. As Ricky glanced her way again, he caught Lexi's eye. She smiled once more, and he got even more motivated to find a way to spend just five minutes alone with her.

The hours went on and the sky darkened in response. A big white sheet served as a makeshift screen and a movie began playing from a projector. Groups of kids started to form in various places around the yard, some sitting to watch the movie, others laughing and talking about their summer and the upcoming school year. Lexi was visiting with some friends too far away for Ricky to overhear the conversation, but close enough that he could see the way her nose crinkled when she laughed. Ricky sat down on a blanket next to Liv, Leah, and Emily, using the movie as a distraction while he tried to formulate a more concrete plan. He still hadn't told Lex how he really felt, and time was running out.

The party was coming to a close and the majority of kids decided they were ready to call it a night. A small group of stragglers opted to head over to McDonald's for a late-night food run. Never one to turn down fries, or extra time with Lex, Ricky joined the food going group.

"Hey Lex, you want to ride over with me?" he said, flashing her a smile.

"Sure!" she said, the thought that she was sixteen and could now officially date had not left her mind once all day.

Lexi had promised herself that she would not have a boyfriend until she was sixteen years old. That didn't mean that she had never had strong feelings for a boy before or that she hadn't found herself on the silent end of a crush. It just meant that she had made herself a promise that she wanted to keep. Now here she was finally old enough to experience the emotions she had been feeling for the past few months, and her best friend—whom she could one day possibly see as more than a best friend—was asking if she wanted to ride to McDonald's with him. This was turning out to be the stuff movies were made of.

Everyone began piling into cars. Lexi hugged Kris and Emily goodbye. Ricky found a rogue soccer ball and began dribbling it back and forth between his feet.

"Hey, how much do you want to bet that I can hit that volleyball pole with this soccer ball?" Ricky said to Lexi and Emily with a challenging grin on his face. Emily knew he was self-assured and wasn't sure if he was just trying to show off or if he was actually capable of the shot. She decided to call his bluff. She had yet to meet a basketball player that was an accurate soccer player.

"No way you're hitting that," said Emily. "It's getting pretty dark and that thing is at least twenty yards away."

Ricky wiggled his dark eyebrows up and down as his grin broadened. "What will you give me if I do?"

"I'll buy you McDonald's if you actually hit it, but I don't think you can. Do you realize how far away you actually are?"

"McDonald's?" Ricky said, undeterred.

"McDonald's," Emily confirmed.

Lexi was watching the exchange with enjoyment. She loved how effortlessly Ricky seemed to fit into her family. He seemed to freely fit into every part of her life.

Without hesitation and with perfect form, Ricky leaned back and kicked the ball sending it sailing through the air. It glided perfectly until it collided with the volleyball pole. Ricky looked at Emily in triumph. Realizing she may have just been hustled, Emily looked at

Ricky with one eyebrow raised and a skeptical smile as she waited for an explanation.

He shrugged his shoulders and grinned deeply at Lexi.

"Have I never told you guys that I played soccer for twelve years? I started playing when I was four and it was my primary sport until I was eleven. I only stopped playing last year to focus more on basketball." Emily shook her head with a laugh at the knowledge that she had definitely been hustled, and gave them both enough money for McDonald's.

Lexi got into Ricky's car and, to her delight, Drake was playing. The music transported her back to the day she met Ricky, just five short months ago. In some ways it seemed like just yesterday that he had made her laugh by dancing in the clinic hallway at the hospital. In other ways, it felt as if they had always known each other. Having Ricky near felt normal, natural. Ricky felt like the lost piece in the puzzle of her mixed up jigsaw life.

Ricky and Lexi met up with her friends at McDonald's and the small talk and laughter of the night continued. As was always the case, Ricky fit in flawlessly. His spirit animal must have been a chameleon, Lexi thought, because he seemed to change and adapt to whatever situation he found himself in. He was easily liked and had no issues winning over the hearts of a crowd. Lexi contributed to the conversation, while taking in Ricky's interactions with others. Slowly Lexi's friends began leaving the restaurant a few at a time and Ricky and Lex decided to head back to the place where the party was being held to see if they could help clean up.

Kris and Emily were just boxing up the last of the leftover food into the truck as Ricky and Lexi pulled up.

"Do you guys need help with anything?" Ricky asked. He didn't feel as if he had completely won Kris over yet and was willing to do whatever it took to get Lexi's dad to like him.

"We just need to go get the van to load it up," Kris said. He then added with a teasing smile. "You guys showed up just in time to help us pack up and unload."

"Can I walk home to get the van and then drive it back?" Lexi said with a huge grin. She hadn't been a child for awhile now, but Kris knew when she looked at him and smiled like that she would always be his little girl.

"You don't even have your license yet and it's dark outside," he countered, trying to keep his defenses strong.

"It's only five houses down the street and Ricky will go with me, won't you?" she said, looking up at Ricky with a smile.

Ricky all but jumped at the chance of finally getting some alone time with Lexi, even if it would only be for a few moments. Perhaps he hadn't missed out on his chance after all. "Yeah! I'll go with you," he said looking all too eager and then turned back to Kris and added, "Don't worry, I'll keep her safe."

"Mmm hmmm" Kris said, not quite sure if his worry should be more about his car or his daughter. Kris was a natural judge of character. He was able to look upon a person's countenance and get a good feeling for their intentions—a trait that had served him well with three beautiful daughters. He had heard a lot about Ricky Stafford over the past few months. He knew that Ricky had spent a lot of time checking on Lexi and visiting her in the hospital. He hadn't had many interactions with the young man, so he took his lead from Lexi. Kris's oldest daughter was much like him—very reserved when it came to feelings. Lexi loved completely, but she was not one to open up to just anyone. When she let someone into her heart, they were there to stay.

Kris watched as Lexi and Ricky walked side by side down the street. Lexi seemed completely comfortable around Ricky. Kris knew that Ricky meant something to Lexi by the way she spoke of him, but where were Ricky's thoughts? What were his intentions? Lexi deserved to receive the same type of genuine love she gave to others. With everything she was going through right now, the last thing he wanted for his daughter was a broken heart.

Ricky and Lexi walked down the street side by side, close enough to hold hands but never quite touching. The electricity between them was palpable but their nerves won out. Instead, they opted for comfortable conversation, each with a hand straight down to their side, just in case the other decided to take the chance. Once they arrived at the house, Lexi went inside to get the keys while Ricky worked on the timing of events. It wouldn't matter if he had hours, he wouldn't have been able to settle on a plan. Why was he so nervous? Girls had never made Ricky this nervous. Of course, Lexi wasn't just a girl he could smile at and flirt with and she'd fall in love.

Lexi returned with the keys and they got into the white minivan. She carefully buckled her seat belt, silently said a prayer, and took a breath. This wasn't the first time that she would be driving, but it would be the first time that she was driving with Ricky sitting in the passenger seat. Her heart was racing. She tried to play it cool. She exhaled and looked over her shoulder to be sure that no one was walking behind the car, before putting the car in reverse. The coast was clear, so she tried to put the car in gear. Nothing happened. Flustered that she was a little weaker than she realized, she tried again but it wouldn't budge. She didn't remember it being this hard to put a car in reverse. A small giggle escaped Ricky's mouth and she looked over to see him stifling a laugh.

"What's so funny?" She blurted out.

"Lex, you have to start the car before you can put it in reverse," Ricky said, doing his best to not burst into laughter.

"Oh, right," she said, instinctively smoothing her bald head. If she would've had hair now is the time she would have been playing with it nervously trying to brush off the blunder. Any hopes of impressing Ricky with her driving skills were quickly dissipating.

"Well, I knew that, but I just got nervous," she said matter-of-factly as she did her best to simultaneously pick up her pride and start the car.

Ricky smiled and decided to try his game.

"Why do I make you so nervous Lex?" he said.

By now she had successfully started the car and they were slowly going down the street at a steady 5.2 miles an hour. Lexi looked as if she could eat off of the steering wheel. She was so determined to not mess up again that she had one foot on the gas and the other ready to slam on the brake at any moment. Just as a precaution she touched the pedal every other house to be sure that it worked if the situation arose. Her vigilance paid off and they safely made it to their destination. With great effort she parked the car and realized that Ricky had asked her a question and was waiting for an answer. She turned off the car and looked over at him.

"It's not just you. I haven't been able to drive since I was diagnosed because of all of the medications and everything. Plus, you remember what chemo does to your brain; I was worried I was going to forget how to drive."

Ricky's shoulders slumped a bit. That wasn't how he saw their conversation going. Leave it to Lex to keep things logical when he was trying to flirt with her.

"But having you in the car just made me more nervous," she added with a teasing smile.

And I'm back in the game! Ricky thought to himself. It might have been small, but a win is a win and he would count it. The plan was back on and Ricky would have to move fast if he was going to execute it. He knew he wouldn't get much alone time with Lexi, especially now that things were wrapping up at the party. Her parents were still talking with the neighbors that had hosted the party. This was his chance, and he knew it. Lexi got out of the car and Ricky followed suit. She walked around to the back of the car where Ricky met her.

"That was some pretty nice driving there," he said with a small laugh.

"Be nice," she said with a mocking frown. "I told you I haven't driven for a while. Plus, it's my birthday. You should always be nice to people, but especially on their birthday."

"You're right," he said as he put his arm around her, and half hugged her shoulders. "I only tease you because I love you." The words slipped out so easily that Ricky didn't have time to catch them. Instead, he quickly added, "but not the gross way."

Lexi laughed and leaned into his side as she smiled. She comfortably put her arm around his waist. "I love you, too, Ricky. But, not the gross way." Her heart was filled with the warmth from his embrace. She was so glad he had come down and stayed after everyone had left. There was something about having Ricky around that put her at ease, at least when motor vehicles were not involved.

Just then Cam, Liv, and Leah came around the corner of the house carrying the leftover food, coolers, and party decor. Ricky exhaled and unwillingly took his arm from around Lexi's shoulder. He went to help put away the remaining tables while Lexi said goodbye to the neighbors. Everything was loaded and Kris and Emily piled into the van with Cam, Liv, and Aleah. They made the short drive down the street to their house. Ricky had offered to take Lexi home, hoping for his chance to finally tell her how he really felt.

Ricky and Lexi pulled up to her house and talked for a few minutes. Ricky could tell that the events of the night were beginning to take their physical toll on Lexi's body. She was looking tired, but she didn't seem to be in any rush to go inside. They got out of the car and walked side by side to the front door. Ricky stood facing Lexi and decided he had waited long enough. He mustered his courage and went in for a real hug. This was not the first time that he had hugged Lexi, but it was the first time that he had allowed himself to start understanding his feelings for her. He wrapped his arms around her small frame and held on longer than he ever had before.

"Thank you for inviting me tonight," he said softly as he held her. He could feel her smile against his chest.

Lexi's head came to rest just below Ricky's chin. He marveled at how comfortably Lexi fit into his arms, as if he were created for the sole purpose of holding her. As Ricky pulled her closer, Lexi felt her face flush and she was grateful it was dark outside. Was this the moment she had been waiting for? Was she really about to get her first kiss on the night of her sweet sixteen birthday party, by her best friend? Her stomach felt like it used to after having front-flip contests with her cousins on the trampoline. She was certain that Ricky could hear the reverberations of her heart.

Ricky leaned back slowly but kept Lexi in his arms. He looked at her, really looked at her. She was breathtaking. In every possible way, she was beautiful. He wanted nothing more at that moment than to bring his lips to hers and kiss her. Everything in him wanted her. But, without warning a thought came to his mind as clear as a friend offering sound advice. *You don't want her thinking this is all that you want. She isn't like other girls. You don't want to be just another boy to her.* You still have a lot to learn before you are ready to date her. Ricky tried to brush the warning off as nerves that were just trying to provide a reason to chicken out of his plan, but it was no use. He knew what he had to do, even more, what he wasn't ready to do. Ricky looked at Lexi again. She wasn't the kind of girl that you kissed just once. She was the kind that you would want to kiss forever, to be with always.

Yes, she was beautiful, but Lexi was so much more than that. Ricky didn't want to be just another guy trying to date her. He wanted to be special to her like she was to him. He knew that as much as he wanted to, he wouldn't kiss Lexi tonight. He dropped his arms and saw the confusion of his own heart reflected in Lexi's crystal eyes.

Ricky made small talk for a few moments asking Lexi about her upcoming treatments and plans for school—all things they had previously discussed. Then he hugged her once more. This time Ricky knew he wouldn't try to kiss her. Instead, he tried to convey his emotions through his embrace. He held Lexi and silently prayed she might understand the unspoken message he was trying to send. Lexi basked in the comfort of Ricky's embrace and marveled at his ability to put her soul at ease while causing her heart to perform backflips. They stood holding onto one another while their hearts tried to say what their words couldn't. Their time had not yet come and somehow they both knew it. They needed one another but not in this way, not yet. Ricky let Lexi go, then he got in his car and drove home.

The drive back to Provo seemed a lot longer than the drive to Magna. Ricky felt at peace knowing he had made the right decision in not kissing Lexi, but it didn't mean that the desire to kiss her had vacated. If anything, tonight had solidified what he had been suspecting for quite some time. He took a deep breath in and slowly let it out. Lexi had just barely turned sixteen and he still needed to finish high school, serve his mission, and start college. Maybe Lexi was just a crush—and if that were the case, he could quickly get over her. But, he knew that wasn't the case. He had experienced crushes before. A sense of urgency generally accompanied a crush, a need to strike before the flame of excitement was extinguished. What he had with Lexi was lasting. There was no need to rush, only to nurture and protect. He knew that what he had with Lexi needed to be safeguarded and that he had a lot of learning and growing to do before he was ready to start dating her.

"Hey sis!" Emily said, as Lexi walked into the house. "Is everything okay? You look a little confused."

"Yeah, I'm good," Lexi responded. "Boys are just the weirdest."

Emily let out a small laugh in agreement and asked what happened.

"Nothing, that's the problem," Lexi said somewhat bothered.

After seeing the confused look on Emily's face, Lexi continued. "Okay, best friend mode," Lexi said.

"Best friend mode," Emily repeated, knowing their conversation had switched from mother-daughter to friends.

"I thought for sure that Ricky liked me and was just waiting until I turned sixteen to ask me out. Then I thought that he was definitely going to kiss me tonight. But, no! He just kept hanging around and hugging me. He hugged me good night three separate times, Mom. After the second one I thought he was definitely going to kiss me and I was completely ready for it, I think. He stared at me for a long minute and then stepped back like he needed space and started asking me how radiation has been going and if I'm excited for school to start. Who uses radiation as small talk? Then he hugged me one more time and held on like he didn't want to let go. I know I'm not good at flirting or picking up on hints, but I really thought he was going to try to kiss me tonight."

"Would you have wanted him to kiss you?" Emily asked.

"I wouldn't have minded it," Lexi said. She could feel her cheeks flush even as the words left her mouth. She was grateful that no one else was around to hear her confession.

"So, do you guys like each other?" Emily asked.

"Honestly, I don't know how he feels. I thought I understood him but I'm just not sure anymore," Lexi answered.

"How do you feel?" Emily asked.

"I don't know. I'm barely sixteen. He's my best friend." Lexi paused for a moment and then added, "It's hard to explain everything I feel for him. I just know that I feel better when he's around." Lexi blew her breath out in an effort to clear her head and regain control of her heart. "Right now, I'm just tired. It was a great party, Mom. Thank you so much for everything. You guys are the best. I'm going to go to bed. Love you, good night."

"Good night, sis. I love you," said Emily. She watched Lexi walk gingerly down the hall and smiled to herself at the knowledge that her daughter was falling in love without even realizing it.

Chapter 7

"Love is friendship set on fire."—Jeremy Taylor

"Hey Ricky, what's going on?" Lexi texted bluntly. Her newly grown eyebrows were knit together in frustration as her fingers purposefully typed out the text. "You've been acting weird since my birthday party. Are you okay?" she added and sent the message on its way.

She let her mind drift back to her birthday and all of the things she had experienced the past few months. In addition to turning sixteen over the summer, Lexi had completed twenty rounds of radiation and passed another mile marker on her road to recovery. The process of radiation began with Lexi laying deathly still on what looked to be an MRI table. Two nurses talked to Lexi as they shaped and formed memory foam type material around her into a mold that fit her body exactly. After that, a small amount of ink was dropped onto Lexi's skin in five different areas running the length and width of her abdomen. One of the nurses then took a small needle and tapped it through the ink and into Lexi's skin. Before she knew it, Lexi had five "blue freckles." These small dots would serve as markers to help the nurses line up the precise location of where the radiation would be aimed.

For four weeks straight, Lexi and Emily drove to the hospital every day, Monday through Friday. Lexi would change into a hospital gown and sit in a waiting room, filled mostly with women three times her age. Upon hearing her name called, Lexi would follow the nurse to the cold metal slab that held the form of her body. With the assistance of the nurse, Lexi positioned herself inside the form and held completely still. The nurse then disappeared behind a wall in an effort to protect herself from the radiation that was delivered directly into Lexi's bare torso and then reappeared to help Lexi climb down from the table. Lexi would then return to Emily in the waiting room and the two would drive home, just to repeat the process the following day.

To Lexi's delight, radiation had offered her body a much-needed break from the poison and pain that seemed to accompany her wherever she went these days. She knew the effects of radiation would manifest themselves one day, but for now she was just grateful for the brief respite. She constantly found herself running her fingers through locks of her inch long hair, amazed at the rate with which it was returning. It had come back close to the same color it was before, but with more curl than she had ever had. She had even been able to return to school—an experience she didn't realize would be such a blessing.

But, radiation was now a thing of the past and Lexi was focused on moving forward. Today, she was heading back to the hospital to begin her antibody therapy treatment. This particular treatment had been part of a study for the last several years and had recently been released as standard of care for neuroblastoma patients. The premise behind it was groundbreaking. The patient was given an infusion of antibodies that would essentially paint a target on all of the cancer cells in the body. Then, the body would use its own immune system to fight those cancer cells off. But for every upside to treatment, there is always a downside. Antibody was known to cause extreme pain, high fevers, problems with blood pressure, heart rate issues, and wreak havoc on other organs during the week of treatment. The good news is that this therapy wasn't known to carry the lasting effects of chemo and in many cases had proven to be more efficient in keeping some cancers at bay.

Lexi wasn't entirely sure what this next week would hold for her and if she would have the ability to text or be up for a visit so she decided that whatever was going on with Ricky should be fixed sooner rather than later.

Ricky's phone dinged in his pocket. He looked at the small screen and sighed before responding. Lexi knew him too well. It had been only a few short months since Lexi had turned sixteen and although they had continued to text and spend time together, Ricky refused to let himself get that close to kissing Lexi again until he knew for certain that the time was right. He didn't know if he would be strong enough to resist the urge twice in a lifetime. The thought of kissing Lexi caused his cheeks to flush. The feelings he had for her had not subsided, but neither had the distinct impression that he had received that night. Their time was not now. If he pushed or tried to convince himself otherwise, he could mess everything up for whatever the future held for them. This was uncharted territory for him. In every other relationship he had, he had followed a particular plan—charm her, flirt with her, express his feelings, instinctively she would do the same, then he would kiss her. The whole process could take place in a matter of days, weeks if he felt like drawing it out. It was a routine that had proved to be successful. Why fix what wasn't broken? Yet, with Lexi he had clearly been told to wait. He didn't mind, Lexi was worth the wait. He knew how he felt about Lexi but could do nothing about it right now. He pushed his emotions into the pit of his stomach and then willed them beyond that. He knew what he had to do.

"The thing is Lex," he began typing, trying to think of the best way to phrase what he knew he needed to say but didn't want to, "is that I don't really want a girlfriend right now. I just need to focus on school and on basketball and on getting ready for my mission." He breathed out loudly in an effort to convince himself that this was for the best.

Lexi looked at her phone. Her heart fell but she pushed her disappointment down quickly. With a false determination she let out a small breath before saying her response aloud as she typed it.

"Well, that's good because I just turned sixteen and I don't want a boyfriend, Ricky. I want a friend and that's all. If I wanted a boyfriend, I would have one, but starting a relationship right now is not on my list of priorities. I don't want someone who's looking for something else because I'm not ready for that in my life. I want to date and experience life as a teenager. I don't need a boyfriend to do that. I'm sorry if you got the wrong impression, but I really just want a friend, if that's okay with you." She was satisfied with the message but disheartened by the realization that she had misread Ricky's feelings for her.

It made sense. How could anyone have feelings for the sick girl with the boy hair? She dismissed the feelings of self-pity that flooded her heart. She didn't have the emotional strength to tread those waters. Ricky was nothing more than her best friend, that was all, but that was enough.

Ricky read Lexi's text twice, trying to remind himself that he should be grateful that Lexi didn't want a boyfriend right now. Instead, he found himself a little bothered that she wasn't looking to be more than his friend. Did she look at him the same way she did the other guys who had asked her out? Why had she written off the possibility of him being her boyfriend so easily? He didn't understand why the conversation continued to gnaw at him. He knew Lexi could not be his girlfriend right now. But was it too much to ask for her to look at him as possible boyfriend material at some point?

"That boy needs a mission," Lexi said to Emily as she shook her head. "Just because he is kind of cute and funny doesn't automatically mean that I'm like every other girl he knows that he thinks is just dying to be his girlfriend. Why would he think that I even want a boyfriend? I just barely turned sixteen. I don't want to date just one person. I don't want a boyfriend. I want to date a bunch of different people to decide the type of guy I want to marry."

Emily listened to Lexi's small rant while trying to suppress a smile.

"Besides, even if I did want a boyfriend, who says I would want it to be Ricky? Yeah, he's my best friend and he's great and a little cute and has good standards and is always making me laugh and I can talk to him about everything but why does he just assume I'd want him to be my boyfriend?"

"The nerve of some guys . . ." replied Emily, hoping that Lexi wasn't seeing the look of amusement evident on her face.

"At least we have things cleared up and we can just go on being friends and things can go back to normal," Lexi said.

"That's good, sis," Emily said, her voice still thick with mirth.

Lexi's phone buzzed and her face instantly lightened.

"Oh! Ricky just texted again and he's going to come up to see me tomorrow. Is that okay?" Lexi said with a clear change of mood.

"Of course," replied Emily.

Lexi spent the week inside the perfect storm of medication, pain, fevers, and beeping monitors. Nurses paraded through her room at all hours of the night and the recollection of Emily conversing with the doctors in hushed tones had somehow penetrated Lexi's clouded psyche. She vaguely recalled a visit from Ricky in which he may have finally beat her at Phase 10. But, she couldn't fully trust the murky memory so she decided she could retain her undefeated status. Regardless of the tornado of antibody therapy, the doctors' predictions had been accurate. As soon as the treatment was completed, Lexi saw a slight improvement in her body. She was even strong enough to walk herself to the car, with the steadying arm of Emily beside her. Just five more rounds of the antibody warfare and she would be done with treatment and moving on with the rest of her life. Five more hospital stays, and she could leave her four-blue-walled world behind her.

Ricky opened the door for Lexi before walking around to get in his car. He looked at her and smiled as he folded his arms. She followed suit and he said a quick prayer. This was just one of many things that separated Ricky Stafford from the other boys Lexi had dated. Ricky prayed before driving anywhere. He didn't pray to impress anyone. It was just part of who he was and what he did. He once told Lex that it started when he began driving himself to school. The drive was quiet, and it was time for him to just talk openly with God. Now, it was a habit but not one that he took for granted. As the prayer ended, Lexi made a mental note that when she was ready to get married, her husband should be as comfortable speaking with Heavenly Father as Ricky was.

"What do you want to do in life, Lex?" Ricky asked her, bringing Lexi back into the moment. Today they were heading to watch Danja, Ricky's younger sister, play in her high-school volleyball game. Danja had come with Ricky to visit Lexi a few times and the two girls became fast friends. A week prior, Danja had told Lexi that her team was dedicating tonight's game to all of those who had battled cancer. Cancer survivors would be honored at the beginning of the game, and Danja had personally invited Lexi to come.

"I'm going to be a pediatric oncology nurse," Lexi replied to Ricky's question matter-of-factly. "I'd like to go back to Primary Children's to work someday but I know I won't stay there forever. I'm going to be living out of the state for part of my life as well."

Ricky smiled and slightly shook his head.

"Why are you smiling?" Lexi asked simply.

"Most people who have gone through what you have gone through would want to stay as far away from hospitals as they could for the rest of their lives, Lex. But you want to make a career out of working in one. Not just in general either. You want to work in the very place that holds so many hard memories for you. It kind of blows my mind. Why not just distance yourself from all of it? Wouldn't it be easier to try to forget your hard times than to face what you've been through every day?"

"Well, I actually decided I wanted to be a pediatric oncology nurse before I ever got diagnosed. I just had a really strong feeling that it's what I needed to do with my life. Then when I got diagnosed, I felt like it was a sign. Cancer has given me the chance to learn things about my future patients that a lot of nurses might not understand. I have experienced things firsthand. The prompting I had received just made more sense to me once I was diagnosed. I've learned that when tough things happen there are two types of people: those who run from their challenges and those who stand and fight. I've never been a runner, Ricky."

Ricky let out a small laugh, not sure what to make of the perspective Lexi took on life. He had never seen it before. Just when he thought he knew everything about her, Lexi found a new way to surprise him.

"What about you?" she asked. "What do you want to do in life?"

His grin instantly widened as it did whenever he thought about his plans for the future. Lexi worried his face might split in two from pure anticipation.

"I want to finish high school early so that I can go on my mission as soon as possible. Then, I'm going to come home and start playing basketball. I'm going to play in college for a little bit. Then I really want to go back to Germany where my dad played and play professionally over there. That's my ultimate goal. I want to play at the level he did in front of a crowd of people that are all cheering me on."

"Wow!" Lexi said, looking genuinely impressed. "That would be really awesome! Do you think you'd be able to help a lot of people over there if you get the chance to play professionally?"

Leave it to Lex to skip over the part where he was planning on being a huge sports star with thousands of fans screaming his name. Instead, she went straight to the part where he would be able to help others. How was it that this girl always kept him focused on the things that actually mattered?

"I sure hope so," he agreed.

"You will, trust me," she said with such confidence that Ricky had no other choice but to believe her words. "So, what are your plans if basketball doesn't work out?" Lexi asked.

Ricky's brows knit together subconsciously. He knew that playing professional ball didn't work out for everyone, but he wasn't everyone. He had worked and sacrificed too much to this game to be betrayed by it.

"Honestly, I don't know," he answered. "Basketball is what I know. I've never really had a passion for anything else. My parents have always planned for me to go back to play like my dad did. The idea has been there my whole life. I don't know what else I would do if it doesn't work out," he said plainly.

"That would be really cool for you if it works out," Lexi said. "I have just found that life is unexpected so it's always nice to have a backup plan," she added.

"You are absolutely right there, Lex."

"So, what would be your backup?" Lexi asked again.

This girl constantly challenged Ricky. She made him think beyond his comfort zone and in doing so, helped him realize he was not bound to his current way of thinking. Ricky took a moment to think and responded. "I think I would like to go into education, but not to be a teacher or principal. I want to study education so that I can create a program for kids who get sick. It shouldn't be so hard for them to get their education. I'd like to work on something that can help others that way." He looked over to see the pride that was in her eyes as he spoke of helping others. He smiled at her and asked, "So, why do you think you'll move out of the state for a while? Are you just anxious to see some of those island boys?" he said while wiggling his eyebrows. Ricky had done his due diligence and learned that Lexi seemed to have a preference for tan skin and brown eyes.

She laughed and responded, "Actually, I had a blessing that said that I won't live here my whole life so I figured I should get used to the idea now."

"That's kind of cool that neither of us are planning on living in Utah our whole lives, huh?" he said excitedly.

"Yeah!" Lex agreed as the corners of her mouth turned upward without conscious effort on her part.

"So do you think you'll marry one of those island boys when you move there?" he said trying to play it cool, but far more interested in her answer than he wanted to admit.

"Who said I was moving to the islands?" she responded with a half-smile. "I don't really know where I'm supposed to go yet. But, to answer your question, it would take far more than a nice skin tone for me to marry someone."

Ricky liked where this was going. Then again, he couldn't remember a conversation with Lex that he didn't like . . . except for the conversation that he had told her he only wanted to be her friend.

"Okay then, Lex, what exactly would it take for you to marry a guy?"

"You mean like what am I looking for in a husband?" Lexi said with a little laugh.

"Yeah, and don't laugh at me," he said while trying to pretend to be insulted. "You've asked me way crazier things."

"No, no, no, I'm not laughing at you at all, but I have a lot of things and I don't want to just blurt them all out. How about I say one thing I want in my future husband and then you can say something you want in your future wife. That way I don't just ramble on and feel like an idiot. Deal?"

"Deal," he said encouragingly, "but you go first."

"Well," she said, "obviously he has to love God more than anything else—even more than he loves me. He has to put God before everything else in his life. It's really important to me that he has his own relationship with Heavenly Father and then I want to build a relationship together with Heavenly Father too." She waited to see his response. She didn't talk this openly with guys her age about these types of things. Actually, she didn't really talk this openly with anyone her age. It seemed like people didn't really seem to understand her anymore. Although she had always had friends, she had never really felt like she fit in. Mainly because the things that mattered to other kids didn't matter to her. Now that she had cancer, that gap had seemed to widen. But, that wasn't the case with Ricky. She could tell him how she really felt about things and knew he could handle it, even if the conversation got too deep. This is why he was her best friend and why she hoped he always would be.

"Hey, you stole that one from me!" Ricky replied with a big smile. Lexi wondered if there was ever a time that Ricky didn't smile, it never seemed to happen around her.

"That's cheating!" she teased him. "You can't just copy what I said!"

"I'm serious!" he went on. "The biggest thing for me is to marry a girl that has a testimony and will rely on God no matter what is going on in her life. When things get real in life, physical beauty doesn't matter as much as spiritual strength. I want someone who focuses on things that last, not things that are temporal. Before I was diagnosed, I thought that physical abilities were the most important thing. My ability to play basketball wasn't just a hobby. It defined me. That mentality was fine as long as I was healthy, but I had a bit of an identity crisis when I was diagnosed. If I couldn't play ball, then who was I? It was an eye opener for me. I want someone that is more than just their talent, more than just their physical abilities. I want someone with substance."

"Okay, that's actually a pretty good answer. I'll give you that one. But you still have to come up with something original. That was too close to mine." She smiled crickled her nose at him as he rolled his eyes. She really just needed time to think about exactly how much she wanted to share and why this conversation was having such a strange effect on her insides.

"Well, I also want to marry someone who wants to have children," Ricky said. Lexi smiled as the words left his mouth, but she hoped he didn't see just how big it was.

"Now you're stealing my answers," she said. "I love babies and have always wanted to have a family. Family is one of the most important things in this life. I saw a flier at the hospital that says that they need people to go and cuddle the little babies in the NICU so the mommas can get some rest. As soon as I'm old enough I'm going to go do that because I love babies and I think I'd be a great baby cuddler."

The thought of Lexi with a baby in her arms flashed in Ricky's mind and he saw her in a light he hadn't seen her in before.

"How many kids do you want, Ricky Boy?" Lexi asked sweetly, using his nickname to bring him back to the present.

"I'm not really sure, actually. Odds are I might not be able to have any at all thanks to treatment," he said, intrigued by what else he would learn about her tonight. "What about you?"

"Honestly, I'll take as many as God will give me. They said I probably won't be able to have my own kids, either, but I've seen miracles before, so if I'm meant to have my family, I will. If not, my husband and I will adopt. Either way, I'll do whatever I need to do to get my family here. I want to be a momma more than anything."

"That's awesome that you can look at it like that, Lex. I probably won't be able to have my own kids either," he said. "But it doesn't mean you get out of going next." Again, with the quick smile—not that she minded at all.

"I want someone who will make me laugh all of the time, every single day. Laughter is important to me," she stated simply.

"You do have a pretty great laugh," he said. "Especially when you think something is funnier than it really is and you start laughing so hard that you can't catch your breath and you do that weird snort thing but, because you can't actually snort it just comes out as a super awkward inhale. Then you laugh harder at yourself and your nose crinkles all cute."

"Hey!" she said, feigning insult. "It's not my fault I have a ridiculously small nose. Besides, you know I'm working on being able to snort and I think I'm doing pretty good," she said proudly.

"Uh huh," he said grinning. "So laughter is important to you. That's a pretty good one. I want a wife that's genuinely happy, no matter what happens in life."

"For real!" Lexi agreed. "Life is hard, but there is also a lot of good in it. One of my favorite quotes is the one from Russell M. Nelson. It says, 'The joy we feel has little to do with the circumstances of our lives and everything to do with the focus of our lives.' You need someone who can see the good, then she can help you find it when you're having a bad day, huh?"

"Exactly!" Ricky said, grateful that she seemed to understand him so easily. "I also don't want her to be high maintenance or so focused on worldly things that she feels like she has to have certain stuff to fit in."

"I get that," Lex said with a shake of her head. "I've never really understood why people spend so much energy on things that don't really matter, especially when you can lose it all without notice." There was a brief pause as the flash of temporal things they had both lost threatened the conversation. Without warning Lexi went on. "You know what I want?"

Ricky had a feeling this was going to be good just by her tone.

"I want a husband who loves me completely for who I am. I want a husband who will play with our children and make them giggle. I want a husband that tells me dumb jokes because he knows I think they are funny. I know that my life is not going to be easy. I need a husband that I can lean on, a husband that won't run when things are hard. He will hold me when I cry, or listen when I talk, or be goofy if I need to laugh. I need a husband that knows all of my weaknesses and still thinks I am strong. I need a husband who can see me at my worst and still think I'm beautiful because he loves me for me. I want someone that is loyal and honest and genuinely loves me forever. That's what I want, Ricky."

As she spoke, something deeper spoke to Ricky. How was it that this girl, with just a skiff of hair on her head and sprouting eyelashes, was having such a deep effect on him? As she was speaking, the only thought that came to his mind was, *I can be that guy, Lex. Let me be that guy.* He dismissed it at once. Surely Lex looked at him as nothing more than a friend. They had both set their boundaries and neither of them were willing to jeopardize what they had. They were to be best friends; that was all. It was what Lexi needed. It was what he would do.

Lexi threaded her fingers together in confusion. *Why on earth had she felt the need to say all of that?* Of course, Ricky was her best friend, and yes they shared everything with each other but why go into so much detail? He probably didn't even care about how in love she and her future husband would be, let alone want to hear all about it. But as soon as the thought came, she dismissed it. There was something about the way Ricky looked at her when she spoke that made her feel like everything that she was saying was the most important thing going on at the time. That was another thing to add to the list, she thought to herself. *Not only do I want someone that can laugh and play with little Ricky and my other kids, but I need someone who listens as good as my best friend does.*

Her eyes abandoned their almond shape and transformed into half dollar pieces. She was grateful it had gotten dark outside. Why in heaven's name would the thought cross her mind that her firstborn son would have the same name as her best friend? She knew that Ricky's oldest son would carry on the legacy of his name and would become Richard Wayne Stafford V, but that didn't mean that she needed to name her son Ricky as well. She needed to change the subject and fast. Ricky was her best friend. They had both decided that's what they were. That's what they wanted. Why was her mind running away with such crazy thoughts?

"Hey!" Lex blurted out a little louder than she meant to.

"Yeah?" Ricky responded. He wasn't quite sure how long he had been lost in his own thoughts, and was praying Lexi hadn't noticed.

"Wanna stop for ice cream before the game?" she asked.

"For sure!" he said, relieved for the reprieve from the feelings he wasn't sure he was willing to allow back to the surface yet.

They found the closest McDonald's and, to their surprise, the ice cream machine wasn't broken. As they pulled up to pay, Ricky got his wallet out and looked over at Lex. She gave him a half smile as she noticed the twinkle in his eye.

"What?" she said as her grin widened. "I know that look. What are you going to do?" Ricky flashed a quick smile. She had learned that Ricky had one of those smiles that put those around him at ease. That quality alone did not merit naming your firstborn after someone, but it was nonetheless a nice characteristic to have.

"Bet I won't get my ice cream from the guy at the window and smash it in my face before I drive off?" he said with an impish grin. He had found early on that self-deprecating acts seemed to work simultaneously to get some laughs and distract him from his own emotions.

"What?!" Lexi said incredulously. "No way! You wouldn't—why would you even do that?"

"Do you dare me? Would it make you laugh?" he asked, his smile broadening.

"Of course I would laugh because that is crazy. Who does that? You aren't really going to do that."

Just then they pulled up to the window and Ricky paid for their ice cream cones. Ricky calmly thanked the worker for Lexi's cone, handed it to her, and took his cone. He took a breath and without another thought smashed the entire thing right into his face then looked directly at Lexi as she laughed uncontrollably. He smiled triumphantly, knowing that his plan had the desired effect and then drove off, leaving the poor worker wondering exactly what he had just witnessed.

"You are so crazy, Ricky," Lexi said with a disbelieving shake of her head.

"It was worth it if it made you laugh," he replied and they drove to the game, her eating an ice cream and him feeling a little more sticky but a lot more content knowing that Lexi was by his side.

Chapter 8

"And suddenly all the love songs were about you."

"Guess what?" Lexi typed. She already knew how Ricky would respond before his message popped up on her phone. "You got your first kiss?" Lexi smiled and shook her head. Why Ricky Stafford was so interested in who she was or was not kissing was beyond her. She ignored his expected reply and forged ahead with the good news. "The hospital just called, and my counts are holding steady! I don't even have to go in for a transfusion this week."

Lexi had finished her third antibody treatment and been home from the hospital for only a couple of days, but her soul already felt stronger. Her body continued with the lashings that treatment unapologetically delved out. But home is where the air of revitalized hope was breathed back into her war-torn frame. She soaked in the precious moments like a child absorbing every ounce of sunshine on the last day of summer.

Lexi slowly made her way from her bedroom to the front room, grateful for the opportunity to watch TV on a couch rather than a plastic hospital mattress. She held the wall for support and gave a small smile of comfort to Cam who was watching her with concern. He had been on silent standby since her diagnosis and always seemed to be exactly where she needed him, when she needed him. Whether it was a steadying hand to walk, or someone to push her wheelchair, Cam had quietly assumed the role of her personal guardian.

As Lexi's hair had begun to fall out, Cam had opted to let his curls grow longer. He no longer looked like her carefree kid brother that chased lizards and buried grasshoppers upon their demise. His brow furrowed with worry; a crease lined his forehead. His blue eyes, just a shade darker than her own, seemed heavy and overcast. He carried a visible weight on his young shoulders, a weight Lexi would gladly carry for him, except for the fact that she was the reason it was there. The knowledge caused the wind to go from her lungs and she stopped slightly to catch her breath. Cam made a slight move, as if to silently ask if she needed him. She pasted a simulated smile on her face in the hopes it hid her thoughts and shook her head slightly. Their unspoken communication was nothing new, they had been doing it their whole lives. But now they couldn't seem to find the words for what was happening to her, to him. So he stayed quietly by her side and she silently vowed to get strong as quickly as she could so that she could one day lift the heaviness that her brother was carrying.

There was a knock on the door. Lexi made no move to answer it. Her lack of energy in returning texts had stifled much of her social life. This gave the friends she had managed to keep the impression that she was either always too sick to hang out or she was in the hospital. They weren't wrong, that usually was the case these days. It was likely just the home healthcare guy dropping off more medical supplies, anyway. Hardly worth the effort of descending six stairs.

"Hey, sis, can you get the door please?" Emily called from the kitchen. If Lexi didn't know better she would have thought she caught a note of excitement in Emily's voice. Things must be getting really slow around the Gould house if the med supply guy was becoming something to be excited about.

Lex agreed as Emily came in from the kitchen to help her down the stairs. Her body creaked and moaned worse than the stairs of the half-century-old house they lived in. Her limbs worked to remember how to navigate home living once again.

Lexi reached the door a little winded and very grateful for the handrail. She grasped the frame of the door with one hand to steady her. With effort, she used her other hand to open the door. To her surprise, Ricky stood on her front porch holding a green poster and a package of Ramen Noodles. He waited there patiently smiling in the chilly February weather as Lexi's hand clung to the door for support. Her mind was still unsure of what was happening. He broadened his smile and wiggled the poster back and forth encouraging her to read the poem he had written for her:

We've both had bald heads, but now we have hair.
We both have cool scars, but mine don't compare.
We've both been on meds, and as lively as plants.
We both have sweet moves, but you're the one who can dance.
So, come with me Lexi, since we've so much in common.
And I'll make you an amazing bowl of Top Ramen.

Lexi laughed aloud as she finished the poem and Ricky let out the breath he was subconsciously holding in.

"Does that mean you'll go with me to Sweetheart's?" he asked.

"Yes!" she said excitedly. "Of course I'll go with you! Do you want to come in now? You must be freezing out there."

Emily parked the car in the hospital parking lot and grabbed a wagon that had been abandoned by its previous occupants. She began loading the month's worth of luggage and supplies into its plastic frame for their week-long stay. Lexi closed her eyes, inhaled exhaustion, and exhaled purpose. Although she dreaded the pain that the impending treatment held, an elation coursed through her veins like rushing water down a spring runoff. She was nearing the end of this seemingly endless journey. These last few rounds were all that was left between her and remission, between her and the rest of her life. She could do this. She would do this. Mother and daughter walked arm in arm through the hospital double doors. The wagon trailed perfectly behind them, chock full of the essential and non-essential "essentials" one might need.

They exited the elevator and, taking care not to spill any of the carefully balanced contents of the wagon, stepped onto the fourth floor. Together they walked through the ICS double doors and were directed to their room. A young nurse came in and greeted them both warmly as she began hooking Lexi up to the pole she would be chained to for the next five days. The three of them chatted like old friends. As the nurse walked out of the room, Lexi glanced from the pulse oximeter on her finger to the tubes binding her IV pole to her body, once again.

I can do this, she thought to herself. *Just a few more times. I will do this.*

She picked up her phone in hopes of distracting herself. The heaviness it caused in her limbs told her that the medication was beginning to take its toll. She lowered her phone as her eyelids began to grow heavy. The nerve pain began to shoot through her body with jolts of electricity as she clenched her jaw in hopes of controlling it.

"Breathe, sis," Lexi heard Emily say. She slowly inhaled and, with great assay, exhaled. Her jaw tightened once again as she focused on the reason for such a treatment. Each day she would receive this transfusion of antibodies that would target neuroblastoma cells directly and kill them. It was a relatively new treatment and from what she heard, it was known to be rather effective. Her mind began to slip and with it the realization of what she was supposed to be focusing on.

"Take another breath, sis," Emily reminded her. Lexi did so obediently. She hardened her jaw and her focus and continued on. The downside to this treatment was the harrowing pain that accompanied it. Chemo brought on the nausea; antibody therapy brought on the pain. At least she could say that she was experiencing it all.

"I need you to take another breath, sis," Emily said.

In an effort to offset the pain that accompanied treatment, a cocktail of other medications was sent racing through Lexi's body. But finding the balance between enough narcotics to make treatment bearable and being able to breathe on your own was a tricky process. The next five days were sure to be nothing short of debilitating.

"Please just keep taking breaths, love. That's your only job this week. I'll do everything else. All you need to do is just breathe."

Her eyelids were closed but she didn't need to see her mom's face to know that Emily was fighting back tears. She made a mental note to focus on her breathing, nothing more. She would breathe. She would sleep. And she would pray that Saturday would come quickly. The thought of spending a normal day with Ricky outside of the hospital took her beyond the fog of the four blue walls she was currently trapped inside. Her heart rate slowed slightly and her mind began to think beyond the currents of pain running through it. Consciously, she took a breath and thought of the sweetheart's dance and how much fun she and Ricky would have together. She inhaled again and thought of what activities they would do during the day. She felt her chest rise and fall with effort, but realized she had not commanded it to do so. Grateful for the knowledge that the distraction was enough to let her body relax to the point of breathing on its own again, she gave Emily's hand a subtle, yet undeniable squeeze and yielded to an exhausted rest.

The next few days consisted of drifting in and out of consciousness. The medication alone did not take the pain away, but the combination of it and the bed of heat packs that Emily continued to rotate offered enough relief to find short periods of respite. The minutes turned to hours, the hours slowly turned to days, and the days finally equaled the conclusion of her sentence for this round. Lexi groggily watched the last of the antibodies deplete from the IV bag into the central line that led to her heart. She had made it through another battle. She was one step closer to winning this war. If the pain she had endured this past week was any indication of the effectiveness of this treatment, her cancer would never come back. But, she didn't want to think about relapse. In fact, she didn't want to think about cancer at all. She had something much more exciting to focus on.

Today, Lexi would be going home, and tomorrow she would be going to the dance with Ricky. The thought made her smile, but she wasn't actually sure if her face had the energy to do so. She decided not to worry about it and save what little strength she had for the wheelchair ride to the car and the walk into her house. Lexi's body was decimated, destroyed from this treatment. But her heart was still fully intact, and that was all that she would need to rebuild herself once again.

"Ricky will be here to pick me up in about thirty minutes," Lexi said as she listed off what she'd already tucked away for the day's adventure.

"I want to be sure that I have enough supplies for the whole day. I've packed the zofran, ativan, benadryl, phenagren, my sea bands, some peppermint oil and peppermint candies, and lots of the blue vomit bags from the hospital just in case none of that other stuff works." Lexi sat on her bed to catch her breath. The weariness of the small task was evident on her pale face.

Emily came to her side and helped Lexi organize the small pharmacy into her day bag so that it fit smoothly alongside her lip gloss, lightly scented body spray, and sweet-smelling hand lotion. She might be a cancer patient, but she was still a teenage girl.

"Do you know what Ricky has planned for today?" Emily asked conversationally.

"I'm not exactly sure," Lexi replied. "After he picks me up, I think we are planning on playing games with the rest of our group at his house. Then we are going to hang out at his house until we go to dinner and the dance."

"That sounds fun!" Emily said. "Are you going to be up for all of that?" she asked with forced optimism.

Lexi's small frame continued to pack and repack the myriad of bottles and supplies into her brown leather bag in an effort to distract herself from the bile rising in her throat. To the unsuspecting eye, her bag would look like nothing more than a large purse. However, the fact that she sounded like a giant box of Tic-Tacs every time she moved, was sure to give her away. Lexi hadn't quite figured out how to keep the plethora of pills quiet when she walked, but at least she appeared somewhat normal when she was able to stand still. She looked up too quickly and caught Emily's look of concern.

"I'm sure I'll be fine," Lexi said putting on the most genuine smile her nauseated gut would allow. "I'm really excited to just go and hang out with Ricky outside of the hospital. I don't want to be the sick girl all the time. I really just want to be able to go on a normal date with him and have fun. I've been praying so hard that I can have one good day. That's all I want. Just one good day."

"I'm praying for that for you too, sis," Emily said. "I know he waited to ask you because he was pretty worried about whether or not you would be well enough to go in the first place. I'm sure if you are sick that you can just tell him and he can bring you home. You guys have a good enough relationship that he would be fine with that. You tell him everything anyway."

"It's not that I'm embarrassed to tell Ricky if I get sick. He has seen me a lot sicker than I am right now and he still wants to be my friend," Lexi said with a melancholy grin. "It's that I wish I could just have one day of not being sick. Most of my close friends knew me before I was sick. Ricky has only known the sick me, the me that needs help sitting up in the hospital or sends him texts that don't make sense when I'm on too much medication. Sure, we've hung out outside of the hospital and he's seen me on some really good days, but today it would be nice if I could make it through a whole card game without vomiting, ya know?"

Emily exhaled, not sure how to respond to the sadness that her daughter had expressed.

"It's okay," Lex said quickly. "At least my hair is coming back and I have my own eyelashes again so I don't look like Yzma from *The Emperor's New Groove* anymore."

Emily laughed out loud as Lexi brought three fingers from each hand to the corners of her eyes for her best Yzma impression then finished packing for the day. Not long after, there was a knock on the door. Ricky had arrived with their costumes for the dance. He and Maren had rummaged through some old boxes at his grandparents house and found some costumes that his grandparents had worn when they were a young couple. Lexi laughed in delight as Ricky, somewhat embarrassed, revealed that he would be Tarzan for the night and Lexi would be his vine.

"I'm a vine?" Lexi said. "What happened to Jane?"

Ricky shrugged and added, "You'll have to take that up with Nana and Grandpa. These are their costumes."

Lexi smiled easily and picked up the green fabric.

Lexi went into her room to try her costume on. It was a pair of kelly green leggings with a matching turtleneck in the same shade. The ensemble was made complete with an adjustable waist skirt compiled of leaves of different shapes and sizes. She took a moment to catch her breath and regain the strength she'd burned from changing into the outfit. She caught a glimpse of herself in the mirror and blew her breath out in disgust. At first glance it would appear as if the costume fit perfectly, but Lexi still remembered what her body looked like before she got sick, and she couldn't help but draw the comparison between who she used to be and the girl who stood before her.

If the pale skin and dark circles under her eyes didn't scream, "I'm the cancer girl!", the tubing running the length of her abdomen definitely did. She was still on TPN so her line had to stay accessed, something that could clearly be seen in the shirt she was now wearing. It was a siren to everyone who saw her, a beacon that she wasn't just a normal, healthy teenage girl. She was grateful for the skirt as it hid her hip bones which seemed to protrude further after each round of treatment. Her shoulder bones jutted from her skin obtrusively as if they had been trapped inside the dermis too long and were fighting to break free. The longer she stared, the harsher her physical reality became. There was a reason she wore baggy clothes. There was a reason she avoided mirrors. She set her jaw to keep her lip from quivering as she blinked hard. She held her head high and tried to remind herself that she was more than her appearance, as she made her way into the front room.

To Ricky's dismay he realized as he put on his costume that he was a bit taller than his grandpa had ever been. Generally, Ricky took pride in his height, but tonight his height wasn't on his side. The one piece, over the shoulder, leopard print contraption he was trying to put on was presenting its own challenges.

"What are you waiting for?" Emily called out to Ricky who was hiding in the bathroom.

"Uh, I'm not sure it fits me as well as it fit Grandpa," Ricky replied sheepishly.

"How bad can it really be, Ricky? I'm a vine!" Lexi said mockingly. "I thought with the whole women's rights movement I would at least be a person," she added with a laugh.

Just then the bathroom door opened and out came Ricky into the front room where Lexi and her family were all waiting. Lexi's hands went to her mouth, but not before she let out a full belly laugh. One look at her reaction told Ricky that he had left his pride on the bathroom floor alongside his basketball shorts. Rather than racing to pick it back up, he opted to turn the living room into his personal runway and showcase himself as if he were at a bodybuilding competition. This response only brought more giggles from Lexi. Her small nose crinkled and her eyes danced with delight at his goofiness. Her head tilted back with laughter as he struck pose after pose. Who needed pride when he could make Lexi laugh so carelessly? Within thirty minutes they had changed back into normal clothes and were ready to start their adventure.

Walking down the stairs and into Ricky's car took more effort than Lexi had anticipated. Sitting upright for the forty-five-minute drive to his house was exhausting and her body begged for relief as she fought to not wretch in the car. Logically, Lexi knew that she should have stayed home, she even knew that Ricky would have understood. But, she didn't want him to have to understand. She didn't want to hold him back. She wanted them to be friends, and not just cancer friends.

Ricky was healthy again. He was whole. He didn't have to worry about chemo and cancer, or bone marrow and blood counts. He could laugh, run, and go to school every day. As much as she wanted it to be, that wasn't her world right now. Sometimes she wondered if it ever would be again. Lexi scolded herself for the internal dejection. She had learned months ago that self-pity was a dark hole that held nothing but quicksand. Rather, she strived to accept the challenges that each day brought and look for the good that came her way. Today that good came in the fact that she would be spending the whole day with her best friend, and she was determined not to let anything—even cancer—get in the way of that.

They made it to Ricky's house and Lexi kept her bag of medical supplies handy as she greeted each of Ricky's friends and their dates. The group consisted of five couples. She recognized many of the guys in the group as being on the basketball team with Ricky. A few months ago, Ricky had brought his team to visit her at the hospital. That had been a good day as she had been able to get to know some of Ricky's friends, while seeing him in a new setting. As Ricky continued with the introductions, Lexi was also grateful to see that she recognized one of the girls in the group as Ricky's cousin, who greeted her with a warm hug.

The games began and Ricky, ever the competitor, was surprised when he realized that winning wasn't the only thing on his mind. He couldn't help but continue to glance at Lexi to make sure that she was doing okay. Something told him that she was not doing as well physically as she had led him to believe. She saw him looking at her and she smiled her practiced smile at him before turning her attention back to the others and the game. He wasn't exactly sure how she did it. He knew from the details that he had overheard at the hospital that Lexi had gone through things that few people would ever experience, but she didn't seem bothered by her trials. She never used them as a way to get attention or draw sympathy. It was a unique trait that mesmerized him.

Something about her drew him to her. Her very spirit was stunning. He felt the need to be in her orbit. And now she was here, in his house, on a date with him, and he wanted nothing more than to keep her completely safe. Ricky had a desire to impress and protect her, although he was unsure how to adequately accomplish either task. Surely, Lexi would not impress like other girls. And, protect? How do you protect a girl from a monster only she can defeat? His mind whirled with a hundred questions he wondered if he would ever have the answers for. Lexi glanced up at him and his heart burned to know what was going on behind those blue eyes.

The games finished and the group went home to prepare for dinner and the dance. Ricky put on a movie to pass the time until they returned. Ricky was the oldest of eight kids, seven of which were boys, and Lexi loved seeing how he interacted with his family. The kids, excited that they got to take part in some piece of the date, found their spots in the family room and settled in to watch "Trolls" with Ricky and Lexi. Despite her quiet pleadings, Lexi had accepted that the nausea would not be held at bay. She had used up any free pass for the day. They settled in to watch the movie. Till, the youngest of the Stafford tribe, took up residence right next to Lexi. She naturally put her arm around him. He cuddled in close to her and quickly dozed off. Lexi began to grow more bilious. She gently laid Till down and leaned over the side of the couch.

"Are you doing okay?" he asked worriedly.

"Oh yeah, I'm fine," she casually responded. "I'm just due for some more Ativan. It's been two hours since the Zofran." She was on a rotating schedule of anti-medics every two hours and she was still holding out hope that this schedule coupled with her sea bands and peppermint might offer enough relief to get her through the day . . . or at least the movie. The effects of antibody should not be holding on this long.

"Oh, okay," Ricky replied, not fully believing that she was doing as well as he hoped or she claimed. It wasn't that he cared about having her healthy enough to keep up with the rest of the group; it was that he hated seeing her sick. She deserved more than this. She deserved a break from cancer. She deserved to have her life back. Lexi saw the concern in his eyes and grinned at him with such a calmness that it put him at ease.

"I'm really okay," she said. "I'm just going to watch the movie and rest until it's time to go to the dance if that's okay."

"Yeah, for sure!" he responded. "Heck, I might even fall asleep. I've been so tired lately. But if I doze off and you need anything at all, just wake me up, deal?"

"Deal," she said easily.

As time progressed, so did the nausea, until Lexi could tell it would not be contained much longer. She silently shook her head, annoyed at her inability to will her stomach to work properly. She ventured a glance at Ricky. To her relief, he had fallen asleep at the other end of the couch. He looked so peaceful, she thought. Then, she said a silent prayer of gratitude that he wouldn't see her vomit as she quickly reached for one of the handy blue bags she had packed. Despite the number of times that Ricky had seen her vomit, he had yet to grow accustomed to it. He didn't get disgusted by it, he understood it was a side effect of treatment. Rather, his eyes grew serious and he looked at her with such concern that she worried if he kept hanging around while she was so sick he may develop an aneurism well before he turned twenty.

Maren had been alternating between working on the computer and quietly observing the situation that was unfolding in her family room. She had known Lexi for about a year now. She seemed like an average teenage cancer girl. She was quiet, kind, and polite. She liked to smile a lot and seemed to think that Ricky was pretty funny. But, none of that could account for the feeling that seemed to accompany Lexi wherever she went. Maren mulled over the emotions that seemed to assault her psyche all at once. She had watched Lexi throughout the day. She didn't know her before cancer, but she knew the cancer life well enough to know that Lexi's body was not doing well today. Lexi had lost weight since the last time Maren had seen her, she was trying to hide it, but it was evident in the hollows of her cheeks and the dark circles under her eyes.

Just then, the crinkle of plastic broke through Maren's thoughts. Surprised, she looked around the computer to see Lexi vomiting without a sound into one of the same types of bags that Ricky used to use. There was no fanfare, no rush to make it to the bathroom in a panic. Lexi quietly sat at the edge of the couch until she had expelled the traitorous contents of her stomach. Ricky quietly slept through the whole ordeal. Maren silently took the scene in as she struggled to process her thoughts. Exactly how sick was this girl? Was spending the day with Ricky, surrounded by a bunch of rascally kids going to compromise her health further? Should Maren step in and demand that Ricky take Lexi home at once? Maren began to feel as if she had underestimated the full weight of the character of this young woman. She had always seen Lexi as Ricky's frail cancer friend, but it was clear she was much more. The questions began to trickle in one at a time, slowly at first, but the flood gates quickly began to open.

Lexi wasn't just the type of girl that someone had a crush on for a while. She was different. She had substance, an unspoken strength that accompanied her. She wasn't loud and ostentatious. She was quiet and reserved, a deep ocean as opposed to a babbling brook. One could be in Lexi's presence for long periods of time without tiring of her company and yet she did nothing to seek out the attention of others. Maren was beginning to understand more of who Lexi was, but why would this girl risk coming here today when she was clearly still so weak from treatment? Did Lexi have feelings beyond friendship for Ricky? Was Ricky aware of those feelings? If so, did he have those same types of feelings for her? Maren subconsciously shook her head in an effort to gain perspective. Ricky was a charmer. He always had been. He was not a fan of being alone. He was known to ask girls on dates or befriend others simply because he enjoyed the company, but from what Maren had heard, Lexi was going on plenty of dates with guys from multiple schools. Had Ricky asked Lexi on this date as a way to be nice to the cancer kid or because he actually had feelings for her? Maren turned back to the computer as she tried to comprehend the tip of an iceberg that she never realized was coming.

Lexi glanced at Ricky to be sure that he was still asleep. His little brothers had long since abandoned the thought of sitting still for a movie. Till had unceremoniously been woken up with a dogpile of brothers. After a quick scuffle followed by a warning glare from Maren, the boys retreated to the great outdoors to rediscover whatever adventures awaited them in their own backyard. Lexi felt the bile she'd been holding at bay rise again in her throat. Her supply of blue vomit bags was almost extinct and she still had dinner and the dance to attend. Perhaps if she could make it to the bathroom she could expel the nausea for at least a few hours. She slowly forced her slender legs off of the couch and felt the weakness that followed from the physical exertion. She placed her hands on the couch and with complete assiduity raised herself up. With leaden steps she shuffled towards the bathroom, praying that she might make it in time.

Lexi lowered herself towards the floor, aware that the effort of standing and vomiting was a luxury she did not currently possess. The retching came almost instantaneously. Her most recent anti-nausea medications floated in the sea of stomach acid, as if to mock her for thinking she could avoid this fate. The cold sweat on her forehead sent shivers down her spine as another round of regorging entered the porcelain bowl. She moved as if to leave and her stomach lurched once more.

"The object of prayer is not to change the will of God, but to align our will with His." The words that her parents had taught her a thousand times growing up played through her mind as she tiredly held her head over the bowl. Her body emitted what was left of its contents. The evidence that she was not meant to have one "normal" day, despite her prayerful pleadings, continued to be projected into the porcelain bowl. When nothing was left, the unproductive dry heaving began. How much longer would she be a prisoner to the medication she had received?

Emily's phone dinged signaling a new text. She wouldn't be surprised if it was Lexi asking for another idea to help with the nausea. Maybe she had finally given in to the sickness and was coming home. They both knew she was too ill to go to the dance. But to Emily's surprise it wasn't Lexi's number that popped up on her phone.

"Hi Sister Gould, my friend is really sick and I don't know how to help her. What can I do?" Emily could feel the helpless desperation in Ricky's words. She didn't have a chance to respond before another text came across, this one from Maren.

"Hey, this girl of yours is not doing so well. She says she is okay, but I'm not so sure. What are your thoughts?"

Not a moment later, a third ding signaled a text from Lexi.

"Hey momma, do you think it would be okay if I asked Rick, Ricky's dad, for a blessing? I really want to be well enough to stay and finish the date but right now my body is getting worse and the medicine is not helping."

Emily responded to Lexi's text first and they talked about the risks and benefits of finishing the night as planned. Lexi expressed her desire to stay and make the most of a "normal" date with Ricky. Then they talked about the miracles and peace that had accompanied priesthood blessings she'd been given in the past. Lexi made the decision to ask for a blessing and then follow the promptings that came with it. She was at a loss and could no longer force her will. It was time to understand what God's will was. Surely there was a reason for what she was going through.

"Thank you" Lexi said with a smile after Rick had taken his hands from her head following the blessing.

"You're very welcome, Lex," Rick said as he put his arm around her shoulder and hugged her. "What's the plan now for you two?" he asked looking from Lexi to Ricky.

Ricky looked at Lexi and asked, "How are you really feeling? Do you want to just stay here and rest, head home, or try to go to the dance? It's completely your call."

"I'm doing okay. I'd really like to try to go to the dance. I think it would be so fun and I'd like to meet more of your friends," Lexi said with a smile.

"As long as you're sure that's what you want to do," Ricky said. "Then that's what we'll do. I'll go put on my Tarzan costume and hope

I don't get dress coded for those shorts. Seriously, how did Grandpa ever wear those?"

Maren and Lexi laughed as Ricky quickly jogged up the stairs and into his bedroom to change. Lexi slowly walked to her bag and pulled out her fitted green costume with the leaf skirt. She walked into the closest bathroom, silently vomited again, and changed into her outfit for the night. She glanced in the mirror and couldn't help but notice once again how her central line protruded from beneath her costume, or the way that her eyes looked shallow and sunken from exhaustion and lack of sleep. She exhaled and thought to herself, *Well, at least you have more hair than your date does this time.* The thought made her smile, and she exited the bathroom.

When she came out, she couldn't help but laugh out loud. There stood Ricky in his fuzzy, leopard print Tarzan outfit once again. The costume draped over his left shoulder and the bottoms had been sewn into a pair of shorts that would have made John Stockton blush. Ricky responded to Lexi's giggles with a shrug of his shoulders and a broad grin, not entirely sorry that the costume showed off his abs. She may not have been aware of them the first day they met, but she was sure to be at least a little impressed with them at least once throughout the night. He had worked so hard to get them back since his bout with cancer, they had to come in handy for something.

"What do you think, Lex? I make a pretty good Tarzan, right?" he asked as he fully extended his arms showcasing an extensive wingspan.

Shaking her head slightly, Lexi said through her laughter, "Those shorts are something else! At least the top shows off your port scar so you don't have to pull your shirt up to impress the girls."

Ricky feigned insult but quickly recovered. "Don't act like I'm not the best looking 6'2" skinny Tarzan you've ever been on a date with."

"You got me there," Lexi said with a twinkle in her blue eyes.

Maren watched them go with a melancholy smile. She knew from the words of the blessing that there was no imminent threat that awaited Lexi if she chose to attend the dance. But, she also knew that her decision would not come without a cost. Maren could not shake the feeling that Lexi was trading any strength she would use tonight for good days to come. In short, she knew that by going to the dance with Ricky, Lexi was deciding to have more pain and challenges over the coming days. Maren didn't feel the need to share her impression with Lexi before she left, something about the deepness of the girl's countenance told her that Lexi already had an understanding of the decision she was making. Lexi would pay the price for one night of semi-normalcy.

They pulled into the parking lot of a nearby building. Lexi looked up at the glass edifice and took a few steadying breaths as Ricky exited the car. He opened her door as she gingerly stepped onto the pavement. She looked up at the towering structure and silently prayed they would be staying on the first floor for pictures. Stairs were out of the question tonight and the thought of riding in an elevator caused her stomach to lurch.

Once in the building, they found a small display of indoor plants that appeared to be set up specifically as the backdrop for their pictures. A family friend met them there and began the small photo shoot. However, the security guard did not find Ricky's costume as comical as Lexi did and threatened to charge him with lewdness if they did not leave immediately. Luckily, they had already gotten a few pictures, so they exited the building without further complications.

They headed to dinner and Lexi was grateful that she was able to sip a Sprite and enjoy the conversation with Ricky and his friends as he recounted the erroneous charges he was almost brought up on. They finally made it to the dance and although Lexi was beyond enervation, she could not help but be filled with gratitude that, against all odds, her body had sustained her this long.

Ricky and Lexi walked side by side into the high school gymnasium. The academic budget coupled with the efforts of the student body officers had paid off. The same gym that Danja had played volleyball in was now filled with balloons, streamers, and a plethora of teenagers in couples costumes. The music blared and the chaperones hung in the corner, hoping the night would end quickly so that they could retreat to their homes.

A slow song began to play, and Ricky looked softly at Lexi.

"Lex, will you dance with me?" he asked as he easily took her hand.

"Yes," she said with a smile that made everything else disappear.

Ricky's hand slid around Lexi's waist. She placed her hand on his shoulder as he held her other hand in his. They fell into silence, not because they had run out of things to talk about, but because the moment they were in needed to be felt. There were no hospitals, no IVs, no nurses, no one else. Just the two of them holding onto one another as the lyrics to the song filled the room and their hearts.

Wise men say only fools rush in
But I can't help falling in love with you.

As they swayed back and forth, Lexi couldn't deny the comfort that she found in Ricky's arms. She had prayed all week for just one day to spend with Ricky. One day without cancer getting in the way. One day for him to just see that she was more than the sick girl. At that very moment, his arms tightened slightly around her as if his soul was trying to reassure Lexi's heart that he had heard the unuttered words she had spoken. Lexi subconsciously moved into his embrace.

The day hadn't been what she had hoped for in terms of her physical health, yet at that moment she was exactly where she wanted to be. The realization startled her. She knew that her life would not be easy, knew that she would always have challenges. She'd wanted so badly to protect Ricky from seeing just how bad those challenges could be. Yet, her prayers had seemed to go unanswered. Ricky had seen her weaknesses, her sickness, the ugliness of her disease. But rather than shy away from her as she had anticipated, he had pulled her closer. She let her head rest on his shoulder as the song finished its melody.

Take my hand,
Take my whole life, too
For I can't help falling in love with you.

They danced the entire song with no interruptions. Ricky held onto Lexi just a little longer than he needed to after the song ended. The night finally felt complete.

The dance ended and they began the drive back to Magna. It didn't take long for Lexi to curl up with the blanket that Ricky had brought for her and fall asleep in his passenger seat. He ventured a sideways glance at her finally resting, completely worn out by the day's activities. He wondered if she was comfortable, if she was warm enough, if she was going to be okay. He wondered how he got to be so lucky as to be the one with her right then.

As he drove, Ricky's thoughts continued on Lexi, how could they not? He had spent an entire day with her. He had seen how sick she was and how hard she worked to downplay it so as not to worry him or draw attention to herself. But her efforts had the opposite effect. Ricky found the more he was around Lexi, sick or not, the more he wanted to be there for her. He wanted her to understand that she didn't need to downplay what she was going through to protect him. On the contrary, he wanted to be there to protect and comfort her.

They pulled into Lexi's drive and Ricky walked to Lexi's side of the car. He opened her door and gently touched her shoulder to wake her and help her inside. Emily had been waiting up to help Lexi with her nightly meds and to begin her TPN. Ricky held his arm out to steady Lexi as she climbed the stairs, his other hand on the small of her back for support. It was clear to see the physical toll that Lexi's body had taken from the day's activities. The strain was almost as obvious as the joy that was evident in both of their faces from being able to spend the day together.

"How was the dance?" Emily asked.

"It was so fun!" Lexi replied with a feeble but exuberant effort. "I'm just really worn out now, but it was worth it." She glanced at Ricky and smiled.

"Did the nausea get better after the blessing?" Emily asked.

"A little bit, but not much. It was more that I just felt like I could handle the nausea better," Lexi said.

"Sometimes our trials aren't taken from us; we are strengthened to bear them," Emily replied, trying to remind herself that there must be a reason for her daughter's continued pain. "It was really nice of Rick to be able and willing to give you a blessing. What else did the blessing say?" Emily asked.

"It *was* really nice of him," Lexi said thoughtfully. "It basically said that I would be well enough to go to the dance but the more energy I used today, the harder my recovery would be for the next little while. It's okay though because it was worth it. I really wanted to go tonight."

"Don't forget about the part where it talked about your beauty," Ricky added quickly.

Lexi smiled shyly and softly added, "That was actually really special to me." Her eyes held the smallest hint of water as she blinked quickly to keep it at bay.

"The blessing said that as I looked around, I'd be surrounded by other girls and it might be easy for me to feel bad about the way that I look right now or my physical appearance." She bit her lower lip subconsciously before continuing. "But I should remember that Heavenly Father knows who I am and He can see my true beauty." Her eyes lifted to meet Ricky's briefly and she quickly looked away.

Ricky looked directly at Lexi as he quickly added, "The blessing actually said that Heavenly Father *and your date* would see your true beauty and to remember how beautiful you are to *them*." Lexi ventured a quick glance up. Ricky held her gaze and she met his soft smile with one of her own. She looked away and tiredly began her nightly routine of bedtime medications and IV nutrition. The monotony of the routine was broken up with the playback of the night's events as Lexi and Ricky went back and forth recounting each activity with fondness shining in their eyes. Lexi hooked her TPN up to her central line. She used her IV pole to help steady herself and stood with great effort. She walked heavily to her room with heavy feet and a light heart.

Maren had called Emily earlier in the week and asked if Ricky could sleep on their couch the night of the dance. She knew Ricky would be late bringing Lexi home and was concerned about him driving home by himself afterwards. The plan made the most sense for keeping both Ricky and Lexi safe. Emily got Ricky some bedding as he changed his clothes and settled down for the night.

The next morning came, and the Gould House was abuzz with everyone getting ready for church. Lexi invited Ricky to come along with them before heading back home. He looked forward to the opportunity to spend more time with Lexi and also size up any local competition. Lexi was moving noticeably slower today and he could tell that the previous day's activities had already taken their toll on her body. He almost felt guilty for wanting more of her time, that was until she asked if she could ride to church with him.

They arrived at the church and Ricky helped Lexi inside. She was doing her best to walk as quickly as she could. With his long legs she knew that he must feel as if he were going at a snail's pace compared to how he was used to walking. However, he didn't seem to be in any rush. He was completely content to stay by her side. They made it to the door and Ricky held it open for Lexi, then she waited while he held it for the people behind her as well. Slowly, Ricky and Lexi made their way into the chapel just as the services started.

It was comfortable having Ricky next to her, Lexi thought, natural even. There was no need for pretense or reason to impress. Ricky's presence put her at ease and somehow helped her feel stronger despite her current physical limitations.

Lexi subconsciously rubbed her hands briskly on her arms to generate some heat. The chapel wasn't cold by general standards, but her body temperature no longer operated on general standards. Without warning, Ricky quickly stood and walked out of the chapel. Emily looked at Lexi quizzically. Lexi returned the glance and slightly shook her head as if she was unsure of what was going on. Moments later Ricky returned with a blanket in hand which he immediately gave to Lexi.

Kris looked at his daughter with a blanket over her legs, and blushing in her cheeks, and then looked past her to the young man sitting next to her. Kris nodded his head ever so slightly in Ricky's direction before returning his attention to the speaker.

Chapter 9

"Distance is just a test to see how far love can travel"
—E.E. Cummings

Ricky took a deep breath as he zipped his suitcase and thought about his life over the past year. He was exactly where he needed to be but not entirely where he thought he would have been. He had graduated high school a quarter early. This was no small feat. Since being diagnosed in February of his freshman year, he had spent the majority of his high school career working to stay on top of his current class load and making up for the time he was in treatment. Long hours of being poked and prodded to complete his assignments had finally paid off. High school—the drama, the excitement, and the stress—was a thing of the past. He had finally closed the chapter on that part of his life, and he was beyond ready to turn the page.

Ricky's thoughts turned to his future. He would be leaving for Boston in the morning. his cancer diagnosis had, in fact, kept him stateside. The next two years of his life would be spent serving a mission for The Church of Jesus Christ of Latter-day Saints. He smiled at the thought of returning home after two years to the applause and smiles of his friends and family after having valiantly fulfilled his duty to God. He thought of which college would recruit him and where his basketball career would take him. Surely, all his hard work—the extra time studying game film, the extra practices, the social activities missed to squeeze in more gym time—was not in vain. He had labored unceasingly to make up the time he had lost to cancer, prioritizing basketball over everything else in his young life. He had done his part. How could he not go on to play college ball somewhere? The thought was ludicrous.

Ricky smiled at all the possibilities that his future held. He could all but hear the crowd cheering for him as he pulled up for the game-winning jumper. How long would he play stateside before returning to Germany and playing for the same team that his dad had won a championship for? He still remembered the sound of the small arena as they cheered on "Rick the Quick" Stafford. He wondered what name they would give him. His heart thumped as he allowed his mind to play over the scenarios time and again.

Ding. His phone buzzed with a text from Lexi. Ricky felt the corners of his mouth turn upward involuntarily. The effect she had on him used to concern him, but not anymore. He had become accustomed to the joy that subconsciously touched his face at the thought of her. He had come to accept it as part of their relationship. He wondered if he had the same impact on her.

"Are you all ready to go?" Lexi asked.

"As ready as I'll ever be. I'm getting all packed and my mom and dad are getting ready for the farewell party tonight. You're coming, right?" Ricky responded.

"Of course I am! I wouldn't miss the chance to tell you goodbye. I'm so excited for you!"

"Thanks, Lex. I'm pretty excited too! I get the feeling that my mission is going to be something that will change my life forever," Ricky said. He tossed his phone on his bed and looked around the room. Tomorrow night he would be sleeping in a new place he had never been, in the same room as someone he had never met. *This definitely will be an adventure*, he thought to himself.

Lexi piled in the car with her family and they headed down to the tennis courts behind Mountain View High School. Today she would officially say goodbye to Ricky for two years. Happiness flooded her mind at the thought of him and a warmth filled her heart. She thought of her life since meeting him. In a very short time he had become a prominent fixture in her world. Her life had been a roller coaster and he had willingly jumped in the seat beside her. Her heart smiled at the recollection of the times he had come to visit, the games they had played, the conversations they had had, the moments they had shared. Lexi's character was solid, but her world was fluid, like Jell-o waiting to set. Her opportunities and plans for the future were constantly changing and shifting in response to her health. Ricky was the constant. He always seemed to be there when she needed him. He wasn't afraid of what she was going through. She could tell him the ugliest parts of cancer without fear of the impact it may have on their relationship.

Flashbacks of the countless hours he had spent by her bedside flitted along memories of the laughs they'd shared over the past year. The life conversations strolled through her subconscious like a child dancing through an open field. Now he was leaving for two years. She would finish high school and begin college. How would life be when he returned? Would they be able to pick up where they left off? Would see meet someone at school? Would he come home and marry someone right away? Would he go away to college? They had vowed to always stay close but was that promise strong enough to actually last? The thought of life without Ricky caused Lexi's rib cage to tighten and her heart to feel heavy. He was the first person she wanted to share good news with and the person who could make her laugh on the hardest days. Was their friendship destined to become a distant memory or did the future hold something more for them?

"Hey, Lex!" Ricky said easily as he walked towards her. He strolled over to her, a gentle swagger in his ever-confident manner. "I'm glad you guys came." He hugged her smoothly and they fell into comfortable conversation. Neither of them wanted to acknowledge the impending separation, both knowing it was inevitable. No more visits, no more late-night texts, no more random date nights. For the next two years they would have nothing but emails to connect them. Rather than focus on the imminent, they laughed without care in the perfect April weather.

Emily opened her inbox to find an email from Elder Stafford. He had been on his mission only a few short months. Emily got his weekly updates along with many people, but aside from that, most of the information on how he was doing came from what Lexi told her. Ricky and Lexi emailed regularly every Monday. If they were both lucky enough to be online at the same time, it almost felt like they could have an ongoing conversation. Today's email, however, was one personally for Emily.

"Hi, Sister Gould," the email began. "How is the Gould fam doing? I sure love you all and pray for each one of you guys every day. I hope everyone is doing good." He continued on, "I have an odd favor to ask. I have a planner that I use each day and I have decided that I want to put pictures of my heroes on the front of it. Seeing pictures of my heroes throughout the day will serve as a reminder to me of the things I have been through and what each of them has done for me in this mortal life to become more like my Heavenly Father. Lex is *for sure* one of my heroes. So, I have a few pictures that I stole from this thing called the INTERWEB, but I don't know if that is creepy . . . So would you mind sending me like one or two that you really like of her? I am not hanging these on my wall or anything for the whole world to see. At least not right now, haha ;) Just for my little planner."

"Ricky wants a picture of me?" Lexi said incredulously after Emily read Ricky's email to her.

"Is it really that hard to believe?" asked Emily.

"It just surprised me. It's not like I have a picture of him on my wall," Lexi said with a small laugh.

"Every boy missionary wants a picture of a pretty girl for their wall," Emily countered.

"Or, is it just because I am one of his cancer friends? Cancer has a way of helping you see what really matters in life. Maybe Ricky is just trying to stay focused on what really matters," Lexi said matter-of-factly.

"I'm sticking with the pretty girl theory," Emily said with a wink.

Lexi laughed good-naturedly and helped Emily decide which pictures to send to Ricky.

Ricky opened Emily's response and his face split in two with joy. Included in the email were a few pictures of Lexi, with the promise of hard copies coming in the mail. Seeing her smile caused a buzzing in his stomach and brought peace to his heart. He almost forgot how stunning she was.

"Who's that?" his missionary companion asked as he leaned over Ricky's shoulder and caught sight of the smiling blue eyes on Ricky's screen. Lexi's hair was a few inches long now and coming in with a soft curl. The sunlight shined on her umber locks and highlighted the splash of freckles that had found their home on her perfect complexion.

"That's the girl I am going to marry," Ricky said with full confidence.

His companion let out a teasing laugh and responded, "Good luck with that, Elder!" as he strode away.

Ricky wanted to be offended, but in reality, knew he was probably right. The longer he was on his mission, the clearer it became. He was completely and hopelessly in love with Alexis Gould. Rather than waste any more time daydreaming, Ricky sent her a quick email, in hopes she might respond before he had to give his companion a turn on the computer.

Hey Lex, How's the fam? How was your weekend? What did you do? How is school going this week? Not that you should be busy in school or anything but if you get time to email me back that would be really cool. Hope everything is going great. Love ya, Elder Stafford

Lexi smiled subconsciously. Getting Ricky's emails made it feel like he wasn't so far away. She quickly responded, hoping to catch him during his limited computer time.

Hi Elder Stafford, I'm great! How are you? Did I already tell you about homecoming? How's the mission really going? I read the email you sent to everyone, but you tend to only tell people the best parts of life without talking about the hard things. How are you really doing this week? I hope to hear from you soon. Love, Lex

Ricky smiled when Lexi's email popped up so quickly. She was online right now and with any luck they might be able to message for a few minutes before he had to go. Although they talked every week, Lexi hadn't mentioned homecoming yet, and he was anxious to hear about it.

You haven't told me about homecoming yet. Let me guess—you got your first kiss? Ricky hit send with a smile.

Lexi read the message and rolled her eyes. Why Ricky Stafford was so concerned with her love life, she would never know. She responded simply.

I got my first kiss soon after you left, haha! I didn't want to bore you with my dating life. I just didn't think it was a super big deal and that you would want to talk about who I was kissing. But, homecoming was so much fun! I got voted homecoming queen and my group was so fun! I went with one of my friends—you might know him because he plays basketball, and one of my other friends was the homecoming king! He is on the basketball team, too, so I think you might know him as well. It was such a great week! How are things in the mission? Are you and your companion getting along better?

Well, that was not how Ricky saw that conversation playing out in his mind. He knew Lexi was dating other people; she had been since she turned sixteen. But the thought of someone else kissing Lexi didn't feel right to him. There he sat in the library, on his mission, next to his companion, while his best friend who he planned to marry was being kissed by someone else. This was not okay. It's not like Lexi knew that he was planning on marrying her, in all fairness to her, Lexi was not really aware of the impact she had on the majority of people—especially guys. This made flirting a bit difficult. In a way he was hoping it would have helped keep her at bay from any serious relationships until he got home. But, maybe someone managed to break down her walls. After all, he had. He decided to assess the situation and see exactly how much damage had been done.

Wait, what? You had your first kiss? Who was it? Do I know him? Are you guys dating? Is it serious? Is he a good guy?

Ricky hit send before he could fire off any more questions. He wasn't sure what he would do with any of the information, but he felt the need to ask, nonetheless. Lexi opened the email and read the barrage of inquiries. She shook her head laughingly, taking note that Ricky had skipped over everything else in the email besides the fact that she had gotten her first kiss. Lexi began her response.

Yes, I had my first kiss. I'm not sure if you know him, he plays football at Cyprus. No, we're not dating. We went on a few dates but I'm not ready for a boyfriend yet. I have so much going on with drill and school. I don't have time for anything else. He is a really great guy, and we are still friends, but that's all.

Ricky breathed out a sigh of relief. He was aware of his feelings for Lexi before he left, but the longer he was away from her, the more he recognized how much he needed her in his life. He knew Lexi needed to date other people, after all, he had. He understood the importance of dating different people in order to find out the type of person you eventually want to marry. In a roundabout way, Lexi dating now just meant that they would be one step closer to being together when he got home. He worked to stay focused on that concept rather than the possibility that her dating could lead her to potentially kiss someone else again.

Something wasn't right. Lexi tried to escape the feeling, but it toddled after her persistently like a small child begging for attention from a disengaged parent. Her body was crashing, her mind spinning. She sat with her team in the gymnasium of a local high school. Her tattered clothes joined an alliance with her false bruises and teased hair. Tonight her drill team would be performing as zombies. *I can do this,* Lexi thought to herself. She tried to focus on the steps of her routine, calculating the amount of energy each move would take. She was back in school full time and was even able to dance again. She loved the exhilaration of performing halftime routines with her team, and even got to help choreograph and dedicate a performance to her small cancer friends. She was healthy enough to hold a job and had started applying for colleges. Slowly, but surely, Lexi was taking her life back. However, over the past few days, she had become miserly with her daily actions, knowing that if she used up her allotment too early on, she would not have the physical capabilities to do what she wanted later in the day. Today's strength allowance was falling quickly, despite her determination to preserve it. She dug deep into her reserves and found enough energy to stand. *Just walk,* she told herself. One foot after the other fought her demands, but she gripped Emily's arm and fell in step with her teammates as they filed out the gymnasium door.

She was out of the gym and heading to the front doors now, grateful that a kind student was holding the door for each of the girls. She was not certain that she could will her arms to push the door open. She just needed to last long enough to walk onto the football field. From there she could conjure up the strength required for the two-minute routine. *Just give me ten minutes,* she said to her protesting limbs. *I promise I will rest all weekend, please just let me have this,* her plea continued. Each step she took brought on a new revolt. Her body was now in open rebellion, clearly dismissing her desperate supplications. She swayed slightly and blinked hard. She recovered before her teammates saw the misstep, but Emily looked at her cautiously. She gave a wan smile, but the effort caused her head to swirl. *Walk,* she commanded her body. *Keep moving.* She took a heavy step. And then another. And anoth . . .

The ground below was hard and cold. She felt her head oscillate as someone placed what she believed to be a rolled-up sweater underneath it. She forced her eyelids to lift. Slowly her vision came into focus and she saw Kris kneeling over her, worry etched deep in the creases of his forehead. His azure eyes were an emotional hurricane of fear and trepidation. Emily stood nearby, talking to someone on the phone, her voice dripping with panic as she looked from Lexi, to the street, and back to her daughter.

"Bingham High School, we're at Bingham High School," Emily said. "My daughter just passed out. She is finishing treatment for cancer and she hasn't been feeling well. Please hurry."

The clouds in Lexi's mind continued to gather as she tried to focus from Emily back to Kris. Her eyelids grew heavy with the effort. Maybe just a little rest would help her feel better, she thought to herself. She surrendered to the impulse and felt her eyes roll as her top lids kissed the bottom ones.

"Lex!" Kris's voice said in terror. "Stay awake! Please stay awake. The ambulance is on its way."

Riding in an ambulance is not as fun as they make it look in the movies. After the paramedics were certain that it was safe to transport Lexi, they strapped her to a board that was less forgiving than the cement she had passed out on.

Lexi's head was spinning. She felt the jostle of the ambulance as it maneuvered through traffic. Her body remained immovable. She was a caterpillar wrapped in a cocoon of straps and wires. Her nose began to itch and she wiggled it, hoping the itch would subside. She watched, detached, as Emily held conversation with the paramedics.

"We've called ahead to let the hospital know we are coming," the paramedic told Emily. "They said that they will alert her oncology team, GI team, and cardiology team. Together they will decide if the surgical team needs to be called."

Emily nodded her head and thanked the paramedic. Emily then turned the conversation to mundane questions about how long he had been a paramedic and how well he liked the job. From her imposed horizontal view, Lexi could see the wariness on her mother's face, the million questions she wanted to ask but didn't want answers for. She saw the pain and the anguish that the uncertainty of her future brought to Emily's countenance. Emily had become a master of diverting the harsh reality they lived in by inquiring about the lives of others. She projected calmness and radiated unspoken strength. But Lexi saw the crags in Emily's carefully constructed armor. She wasn't ignorant to the mascara smudges on Emily's pillow, dark evidence that she cried herself to sleep. She recognized the puffy eyes after a shower that confirmed that nighttime was not the only time Emily allowed her emotions to escape. She often woke to the click of keys on a laptop as the soft glow from a computer illuminated Emily's face as she searched for more information on how to help heal her daughter, or at least understand the constant stream of tests results. She knew all too well the exhale and shoulder slump that accompanied a dead end. The effects of Lexi's disease, her cancer, had spread to her family. The thought caused bile to rise in Lexi's throat. She quickly swallowed it as an involuntary shiver ran the length of her spine.

They arrived at the hospital and Lexi was lifted from the ambulance. Despite the best efforts of the paramedics, the dismount was jarring. Gurneys do not come with shocks. Lexi was carefully wheeled into the emergency room entrance and directly into a prepared room. Having an ambulance as an uber meant that you could surpass the waiting room.

"Now that they have stabilized you, your vitals are looking good, and we got a few x-rays, we are going to start with an EKG to check the electrical function of your heart and then follow up with an echocardiogram to check the mechanical function of your heart. You had the Red Devil and that chemo turns the heart into a ticking time bomb," the doctor said. He wasn't a particularly tall man, standing shoulder to shoulder with Emily's 5'6" frame. His hair was thinning, and he looked as if he was on the cusp of solving a riddle. Tonight, Lexi provided the mystery.

"We first need to be sure that your heart is okay," he said matter-of-factly. His brow furrowed slightly. "Also, how long ago did you break your foot?"

Lexi looked like she'd been caught. Three weeks prior she had decided to work on getting her aerial back. The no-handed cartwheel proved to be too much movement for her frail body to accommodate and she landed unceremoniously on her left foot. An instant stab of pain had shot through her ankle as she gripped it tightly. She had tried to walk it off but had been unable to bear any weight. Emily had come instantly to take her to the doctor. Again, she'd ridden in a wheel-chair. She'd bitten back the pain during the exam and consequential x-rays. She'd smiled and made slight small talk with the nurses in an attempt to mask the discomfort. The Instacart doctor had come in and revealed that her foot was just a severe sprain and that she would heal without a problem. He had recommended keeping it wrapped, but Lexi had figured if it truly needed to be secured, he would've put it in a cast. From then on, she'd wrapped it only when she practiced with her team. She had watched as the foot turned every shade imaginable on its journey from purple to green to yellow. The swelling that had once caused her foot to be larger than her calf, had slightly subsided. But the pain had only increased over the last few weeks. It could have something to do with the fact that she hadn't missed a practice and also participated in a performance only a week after it happened.

"It's broken?" Emily asked, slight irritation for the missed diagnosis evident in her voice. Emily had always protected her children fiercely. But, since Lexi's diagnosis, she had come into full momma bear mode.

"Yeah, it's definitely broken," the doctor confirmed. "It's not yet healed either. With everything else that your body has gone through, it cannot divert enough resources into healing a broken bone. That's why it's taking so long. You'll need to be in a boot for a while," he stated plainly.

Lexi had been in the hospital just three short days. Her official diagnosis was "failure to thrive." The words left a sour taste in her mouth. She worked every day not just to exist, but to live each day to the fullest. Being told that her body was failing to thrive felt like a punch in the stomach. But, the scale didn't lie, neither did the tests. She now weighed only 82 lbs. fully clothed. She continued to will herself to eat, but swallowing was only half the battle. Her body had begun to reject all nutrition and her organs were beginning to reflect the effects of her life-saving treatment. The calories that passed through her lips sat idly in her stomach. Her pancreas had thrown in the towel a few months ago and recent imaging showed that her gallbladder needed to be removed. She sat suffocated by the blue walls. The soft light of the late afternoon broke through the one window in her small room as she awaited yet another impending surgery.

Emily looked over at Lexi who was reading something on her phone. The corners of Lexi's mouth curved softly downward, her brow knit together in subtle worry. The ambient light caused her room to look like the sky at dusk. Her brown hair curled softly in all directions. It was not yet long enough for a ponytail, but too long to be considered a pixie cut.

"How is Ricky doing this week?" Emily asked, already knowing that the two had been emailing for the last thirty minutes.

"He's worried," Lex stated plainly. "He asked why I wasn't in school, and I told him that I have been in the hospital. He asked what's been going on, so I gave him a condensed version. He is really worried about the surgery and how my body will do. He also made me pinky promise—through email—that I would be more open about how I am doing and how things are going." Lex trailed off towards the end as she began typing her response.

I pinky promise I will let you know how I am really doing. To be honest, I feel okay right now. I am frustrated that my body isn't wanting to work the right way, but other than that, I really am okay. How are you doing?

The email popped up and Ricky wasted no time in writing his reply.

I'm glad to hear that you really are doing okay. The hospital is not fun. I'm sorry you have to be in there again. Things here are going okay. Mission life is a blessing, but it is so hard. I feel like people don't talk about how hard it is. It's different from anything I've done before, but it's also really good. I am learning a lot and understanding more clearly the importance of focusing on things of an eternal nature. My whole life I have tried to stay close to God, but also tend to get caught up in temporal things. I'm trying to be better about that. The people here are so good, but it is just really different. I did get to play more streetball this week so that was pretty cool. I'm going to call it prosball from now on because it is a combination of proselyting and basketball. Pretty cool, right? We play pick-up ball with people and if we win, they have to listen to a lesson or come to church. How are you feeling about surgery?

Lexi smiled and shook her head as she typed out her response. Leave it to Ricky to find a way to involve basketball in whatever he was doing. The news didn't surprise her, basketball meant everything to him. She just prayed that he would one day understand that his ability to be successful in life was not inextricably linked to his ability to play basketball.

Lexi groggily opened up her eyes. She found herself in the comfortable surroundings of her four blue walls. It wasn't home, but it definitely beat the sterility of an operating room, or the arid environment of the ICU. Lexi felt Emily's hand holding her own and was grateful for the solace that accompanied it. She heard the familiar voice of the surgeon who had performed her tumor resection surgery the previous year.

"Given Lexi's surgical history, we were unable to do the surgery laparoscopically. You will notice the new six-inch incision below her rib cage on the right side. Due to the impressive way that Lexi accumulates scar tissue, her internal organs are unrecognizable. I did some testing and am confident that we removed the gallbladder. It was in worse shape than we had originally thought. Hopefully this will help her feel better for now. However, it will likely cause further problems with her ability to process and digest food adequately."

Emily's hand never waivered, just squeezed Lexi's three times. Each squeeze stood for a different word. Lexi feebly, but distinctly squeezed Emily's hand in return. *I love you,* Lexi said, without ever speaking a word.

Slight improvements were being made each day. Test results revealed that Lexi's organs were functioning on what was considered normal, given the poisoning they had endured. It was Monday again, which meant that she had another email to read from Ricky.

Guess what? Lexi typed. Only a few short minutes before Ricky's response came through.

You got another kiss? Ricky asked.

Lexi laughed out loud and responded, *No, you goof. I get to go home today!*

Chapter 10

"Sometimes the heart sees what is invisible to the eye."
—H. Jackson Brown, Jr.

If there was one thing that life had taught Ricky Stafford, it was that the more time he spent praying and seeking a relationship with God, the more he received revelation on everything in his life. He felt comfortable with his relationship with God before his mission, but since being on his mission he had come to know God in ways he never realized was possible. From the smallest situations to major decisions, Ricky felt as if God was guiding and directing him. He felt his thoughts transform into prayers as he actively sought Heavenly Father's help and counsel from the most insurmountable tasks to the smallest of topics. It didn't matter what was going on in his life, or where he was, Ricky conversed with his Heavenly Father. In the middle of a lesson, he pleaded with God. During personal scripture study, he spoke fervently with Him. Ricky reached out to God during conversations with his companion. He constantly found himself seeking God's counsel regardless of the situation.

Doors were still slammed in Ricky's face, baptismal dates still postponed, and struggles still ensued, but an undeniable peace filled the entirety of Ricky's soul when he took the time to humble himself and seek the counsel of the Lord. "Look unto me in every thought; doubt not, fear not" had become a mantra which Ricky had patterned his mission after, but the motto was becoming so deeply woven into the tapestry of his heart that Ricky hoped it would serve as a pattern for the remainder of his life as well.

It was Monday, a designated preparation day, or P-day as the missionaries called it. That meant that Ricky and Elder Kendall would need to do their laundry, go shopping, and complete any other mundane tasks that required their attention. If they hurried, they may be able to get in a few pick-up games today. With any luck, Ricky might actually be able to play in basketball shorts instead of the usual church pants, button-up shirt, and tie that he'd become accustomed to. But basketball wasn't the only reason Ricky looked forward to P-days. Today was the day that he got to email Lexi.

Ricky grabbed himself a bowl and poured half of what was left of the cereal into it. He employed the same practice with the milk—taking care to leave enough for Elder Kendall to get some breakfast. He sat down at the old card table they used for a dining table and picked up the Ensign that was lying under some junk mail. He'd already finished his scripture study for the morning and he'd long since exhausted the trivial games on the cereal box. As his eyes flitted from one article to the next, Ricky found himself drawn to the story of a missionary who was sent home early from his mission due to medical issues he was facing. The article discussed the struggles that the missionary faced as a result of going home early and not having the opportunity to fulfill his mission as he had originally planned. Ricky couldn't help but feel a connection to the article, to the missionary.

He shook his head subconsciously. A week ago he had been really sick, so sick that he couldn't bring himself to leave the apartment, but he was doing better now. He just had the flu. That was it. This article was nothing more than random writing meant to pass the time, he told himself quickly. But what if it wasn't? A storm of emotions hit Ricky like a hurricane, but he worked quickly to contain them. He placed the emotions in a box he never wanted to open. He would complete his mission. He would serve the full two years. He was healthy. But, just as he worked to press the lid closed on the emotional box, uncomfortable worry snuck out. This article was placed there specifically for him. The knowledge sank into the undeniable depths of his heart.

His head whirled trying to counter an attack. He was feeling better. He was nowhere near needing to go home. He willed himself to believe that the promptings he was receiving were no more than his mind being overly anxious. He pushed the emotions further inside the box and taped it shut with his flimsy affirmations. He was feeling better. He would serve the full two years. *He was healthy.* He quickly buried the box in the darkest crevice of his mind and went about his day in a futile attempt to busy himself, with nothing more than a myriad of mundane tasks as a distraction.

The hours dragged on as the significance of the article continued to replay in his mind. The emotional box he'd worked so hard to bury resurfaced like an annoying infomercial you can't purge from your thoughts. Hard as he tried, the emotions of cancer pushed through. He allowed himself a deep inhale of fresh air in an attempt to recenter his thoughts. The result surprised him. The thoughts of relapse were ever prevalent in his psyche. However, instead of frustration or anxiety over what was to come, Ricky was filled with nothing more than an overwhelming peace that came from God. He knew he was undoubtedly in Heavenly Father's hands, come what may.

The day passed as the fret Ricky had stashed in the caverns of his mind began their procession forward. Ricky walked down the aisles of the grocery store keeping pace with Elder Kendall as the words of the article hummed in his mind. He washed and folded his laundry and cleaned his apartment to the same tune. It was an emotional hamster wheel he couldn't get off of but wasn't exactly sure how he had stepped on it in the first place. He was feeling better. He would serve the full two years. He was healthy. It was no use. Ricky could no longer maintain the charade. The affirmations he'd used as a defense against his emotions began to crumble.

He sat at the computer and emailed Lexi. The article he'd read earlier whirred in his mind. He composed his weekly email to his family and close friends. The article buzzed in his mind. Lexi emailed back quickly sensing the distance in his words. He quickly reassured himself with empty dialogue. "Don't worry about me, Lex. I am feeling much better. How are you doing? How many hearts did you break this week?" The article blared in his mind.

That night Ricky found his heart intertwined with that of the young missionary he had read about. Regardless of his most humble prayers, the missionary was sent home and never got to complete his mission the way he had planned. Despite his best efforts, Ricky couldn't help but feel akin to the Elder.

A restless night's sleep did not keep Ricky from rising early the following morning. He poured his cereal, grateful that—thanks to their shopping trip the day before—he did not have to be as mindful with his portions today. He began his usual scripture study. He prayed, studied, and focused on how to purge the article from his psyche. He needed something else to center his attention on, something that would distract him from the comparisons that he kept drawing between the young Elder who went home early and himself. He took another bite of cereal and delved further into his scriptures.

Rather than the anticipated anxiety that Ricky expected to accompany his thoughts of an unknown future, he felt nothing but an overwhelming peace. Before he recognized what was happening, pictures of his life during cancer began to flash in his mind on loop like an old movie playing straight from film. He opened the box he had buried deep in his psyche the day before, and simply looked at his emotions curiously. Why did he feel such a connection to an article that had no real bearing on the life he currently led? His mind searched for the needle in the emotional haystack and he allowed himself to exhale the breath he didn't realize he was holding.

Lost in his thoughts, Ricky looked curiously from his scriptures, to his desktop. He felt drawn to a particular drawer in his desk. This drawer wasn't one that Ricky generally opened during his morning study, but he felt as if he were being guided to what lay within its walls. He quietly opened the drawer, taking care to mind the squeak that always accompanied it. Elder Kendall was still sleeping and Ricky felt as if whatever he was about to experience was something that he would want to go through alone. Ricky slowly opened the drawer to see a stack of pictures he had printed of himself during his cancer treatment.

"Look unto me in every thought. Doubt not, fear not." The peaceful feeling washed over him once again as those words echoed through the chambers of his soul. His mind retaliated, firing question after question of what was to come. Yet his heart won the battle. He inhaled with purpose and exhaled with confidence. He was serving the Lord, so the Lord would be sure that he was taken care of, regardless of what the future held. That knowledge trumped any that Ricky could have been given in that moment.

Ricky's feeling of peace had stayed with him throughout the remainder of the day and accompanied him into his studies the following day. It was now Wednesday and he had a routine doctor's visit in just two days. He continued to remind himself that he was feeling much better, he would finish his mission, and he was healthy. But his constant affirmations did not seem near as important as the promptings he was receiving so clearly. Rather than focus on what he thought should happen, he opted to focus on the impressions he was receiving.

As he studied, he received a strong impression to show gratitude for the blessing of cancer. It sounded odd, even to him. Who would have thought to focus on the blessing of something that tried to kill you? But, in the deepest caverns of his heart, he knew that this was something he needed to do. He thought of the mouth sores, the sleepless nights, the uncontrollable nausea, as well as the loss of a social life and his physical abilities. But he looked deeper than that. He needed to use an eternal perspective to ponder on the lessons that he learned while going through his cancer journey. They weren't easy lessons to learn, but he couldn't have learned them any other way, and now it was time to revisit each of them. Happy and sad, he needed to remember. He prayed with an open heart to remember. He prayed to unpack each emotional box that he had safely tucked his memories of cancer in.

Carefully, Ricky laid his memories out in his mind one by one. He allowed himself time to take in what he had gone through. He thought of the days leading up to his diagnosis, and how weak his once strong body had become in such a short time. He thought of the look on his father's face when Rick told him that he had cancer. He thought of Rick's disappointment as he was no longer able to perform the way he had coached him to do. His heart ached at remembering the look on his mom's face, the sorrow knowing that he was no longer capable of doing the things that had given her the most pride. He could see the careless summers, the dreams he had for his future, the plans he had to play basketball, all erased in an instant. He would never again be the same. Maren knew it and Ricky knew by the look on his mom's face that it was true. He looked at the life he now led, so different from the life he once thought he would lead. He thought of the first time he walked into the hospital for treatment.

Ricky's thoughts turned to the impromptu music concerts that he and some of the other patients had held in the halls of the sterile ICS floor. He had sat outside his door and played his guitar or his uke. Before he knew it, he was joined by other patients and their parents. He thought of Danja, no longer a girl, but a strong young woman capable of running a home. He thought of the added responsibility that his disease had put on her shoulders, and the way that she strengthened herself to carry it all, seemingly without much effort. She never ceased to amaze him. He thought of his physical weakness and the insecurity connected to his hair loss. He thought of the times he had felt alone only to realize how close God actually was.

By the time his study hour was up, Ricky had come up with 118 memories from cancer that he remembered as if they had just happened yesterday. He smiled warmly at the memories, with the understanding that his cancer experience had made him who he was. He had spent the last few years trying to put cancer behind him, trying to bury the past. He was realizing that his trials were not meant to be buried and he was not meant to go back to being the person he thought he should be. He could no longer fool himself. There was a reason God had been speaking directly to him over these last few days. He knew why the thoughts were coming to his head. Ricky wanted to serve with his whole heart but he knew deep in his marrow that his time as a full-time missionary was soon to be up.

Ricky woke up the following morning prepared to learn more about what was to come in his future. He poured his cereal (noting that they probably should've bought a second box at the store) and sat down with his scriptures in an effort to be ready to learn what he was about to be taught that day. But the knowledge he was looking for never came. He completed his study, like a typical missionary would. He tracted and taught, like a normal missionary would. He looked for investigators, like a normal missionary would.

By the end of the day, he began to wonder if the revelations of the previous few days were merely just a ruse—nothing more than his mind playing tricks on him. He held to his nightly routine, said his prayers, and climbed into bed, like any normal missionary would. But as he drifted off to sleep, an undeniable thought entered Ricky's mind. *Your time as a full-time missionary has come to an end. It is time for you to go fulfill the other mission that has been prepared for you by the Lord.*

Ricky humbly asked the question in his head that he had not wanted to ask all week. *Is this really true?* The reply was both heard and felt. *Yes.* A melancholy peace came to his soul as he realized with surety that the cancer was back. Transfers were the following day and Elder Kendall would be reassigned to someone else. Ricky would not need another companion. He would be the missionary going home—the Elder who got sick and did not finish his mission.

It was Friday morning, the day of the doctor's appointment. Ricky woke up, got dressed, and put his missionary name tag on. He took a moment to look at his countenance in the mirror, paying special attention to the little black tag that he had worn over his heart for the last eight months. He had planned to wear it for much longer, but knew that wasn't an option for him. He was aware of the stigma that accompanied missionaries that came home early from their missions. Would he become a victim to the same stigma? Ricky remembered the last conversation he had with his dad before boarding the plane to Boston.

"Aren't you going to cry, Dad?" Ricky had asked, fighting back his own tears. Rick hugged him, placed a hand on his son's shoulder and then looked Ricky firmly in the eyes. "The only time you would see me cry is if you came home early because of anxiety, depression, or just not being able to hack it. Don't make me cry," Rick said. Ricky took the advice to heart and swore to never let his emotional baggage get close enough to the surface that it would ever cause his dad to shed a tear.

Going home early had never been an option for Ricky, but now he didn't have a choice. Would he have to fight the emotional demons that had haunted other missionaries that came home early? He found Elder Kendall in the kitchen ready for the day and already eating breakfast. Ricky helped himself to the last of the cereal and sat beside him. They shared some small talk before putting their dishes in the sink and heading to the front door.

The two Elders stopped at the front door for companionship prayer before leaving the small apartment for the day. Although Ricky was certain he wouldn't be returning that day, he didn't want to concern Elder Kendall by packing his things up prematurely. Instead, he plastered his best smile on and gave his companion a big hug.

Elder Kendall looked at Ricky as he opened the door. He stood a solid 5'10", just a few inches shorter than Ricky. His light blond hair was neatly combed, as if even the hairs on his head felt the need to be completely organized.

"I feel like we are in for a long day today, Elder," Elder Kendall said laughingly.

Ricky half smiled back, but it didn't reach his eyes. With a joking tone that mimicked his companion's, he replied "Don't jinx us."

The Elders laughed lightly and headed off to the doctor's office together. The appointment began just like any other—blood pressure, temperature, height, weight. All of the routine stuff. Ricky was pleased to learn that he officially measured 6'3" with his shoes off and weighed in at a solid 196 pounds. He felt strong and athletic. The Lord had been building him up over the last eight months, not only spiritually, but physically as well. Ricky said a silent prayer in that moment, thanking God specifically for the physical growth, as he knew it too, would soon be gone again.

Ricky had become accustomed to these appointments. They were part of the conditions of him going on his mission. As he was not yet in remission for five years he could not be considered cancer free. So, regular tests and blood draws were just part of the package that he signed up for when he submitted his papers. He sat quietly and looked at the opposite wall while the nurse drew his blood. Despite his journey with cancer, and the countless times he had been poked, he had never quite overcome his aversion to needles. The nurse exited the room with the promise of returning soon with a doctor. Ricky was left alone with four blue walls and his thoughts. The solitude was by choice. Elder Kendall had offered to come in, but Ricky had asked for some privacy. He needed time to process the news he was about to receive, time to accept the reality he would be given.

Numbness filled his body and extended through his limbs and into his soul. He didn't cry. He didn't worry. He didn't think about how horrible his life was. He just sat in silence and thought of his time as a missionary. He hoped by some crazy miracle that he would be able to leave these cerulean walls in enough time to go to the baptism of one of their prosball converts, but he knew better than to pray for that. Prayer was not about changing the will of God. It was about bringing his own will into alignment with God's will. The baptism would take place in an hour and a half. Ricky knew without a doubt that his days as a full-time missionary were officially over. He sat alone in silence and mourned his deep loss.

Fifteen minutes later an exasperated doctor came rushing into the room with a look of terror in his eyes.

"I have some terrible news, Elder, your cancer has returned. We need to get you in treatment right away."

Ricky felt no need to cry or panic. This was God's plan. He didn't know why, but he knew that it was. Elder Kendell was hastily grabbed from the waiting room and the two missionaries were escorted into the doctor's office. Elder Kendall looked at Ricky with tear-filled eyes. He placed an arm on Ricky's shoulder and blinked hard and fast, willing the tears to not fall.

"I'm so sorry, Elder Stafford," he said in a husky voice.

Ricky smiled and hugged him. "Don't be sorry, Elder. This is just how life goes sometimes. I've beat cancer once before and I will do it again."

The doctor looked through his thick glasses that sat upon his prominent nose. "You'll need to call your parents, Elder," he said, not sparing any time for sentiment. His gray hair spoke of years of medical knowledge quietly obtained, but his frantic eyes screamed uncertainty.

With a calmness that Ricky knew was not his own, he called Rick. He had managed to keep the tears at bay until he heard his father's voice. Rick had always had a plan for his namesake. Cancer was never a part of that plan, relapse definitely wasn't. Ricky could hear the despondency in Rick's voice as it came through the line. His physical ailment had once again weakened his family. The letdown was too great for Ricky to push down. Unwillingly, he allowed his tears to escape. He did not cry out of fear, but because he had finally accepted what he had known to be true for the last few days. Heartbreak flowed freely from the sea of his dark blue eyes. The blessing of being a full-time missionary for The Church of Jesus Christ of Latter-day Saints was now over.

Rick told Ricky that they would begin making flight arrangements. Ricky listened detachedly. He hung up the line momentarily and then picked it up once more to make the next call.

"Let's not jump to conclusions yet, Elder Stafford. Let's get an idea of what we are facing. I will talk to the doctor and see if there is anything that can be done," the mission president said with forced optimism, but they both knew that the road ahead would not consist of a little black tag.

The call ended and Ricky bowed his head meekly. *Why?* he silently asked God.

Words that were not his own sounded in his mind. *You served your time faithfully and worthily.* It was not a direct answer to his question, but it was what his heart needed to here. An unmistakable peace settled over Ricky once more, clothing him like the heated blankets on the ICS unit.

Chapter 11

"Distance means so little when someone means so much."

"Hey, Lexi Girl" Kris said, his voice thick with emotion.

Lexi looked at the expression on her dad's face and couldn't help but notice how it matched the melancholy tone of the air that surrounded him. His clear eyes were heavy with sorrow and his features were drawn. Lexi's gaze turned to Emily and the water threatening to spill over her mom's green eyes was all the confirmation that she needed. Something terrible had happened. Emily slowly sat next to Lexi on the bed and reflexively took one of her daughter's hands in her own. An uneasiness crept deep into the marrow of Lexi's bones, as if her soul were trying to cry out against what her mind would soon be forced to process. Kris exhaled and lowered himself onto the edge of the bed. His blue eyes, that usually matched hers in clarity, were now clouded over. Worry, fear, and heartache painted the canvas of his countenance carelessly as he took another heavy breath and spoke.

"Maren texted Mom today at work." Lexi watched as Kris paused and exhaled with purpose, willing himself to go on. "She wanted us to let you know that Ricky has relapsed. They just found out. I'm so sorry, sweetheart."

The air went from Lexi's lungs as if she'd been hit with a cannonball at point blank range. She wondered if it was possible to have the wind knocked out of you without experiencing any physical contact. Her chest tightened and her hand instinctively gripped Emily's tighter. She stared forward blankly, unable to register the information she had thought she'd just heard. She must have misunderstood the words that had come out of Kris's mouth. Ricky was on his mission. He had been cancer free for over three years. He was doing what God wanted him to do with his life. He was serving faithfully and impacting lives for the better. She could feel the panic rise as her breathing escalated and she continued to subconsciously list the reasons this must be some horrible mistake. She had emailed him just a few days ago and everything was fine. He was getting over the flu, but he said he was fine. He was supposed to finish his mission and come home and play basketball and live the amazing life he deserved. He said he was fine. Nothing was fine.

"Breathe, sis," Emily said as she slid her arm around Lexi. Lexi instinctively curled into her mom's embrace. The tears fell but no solace accompanied them. She inanimately lay in Emily's arms, staring blankly forward and silently weeping as a deep ache filled her soul. Her parents tried to offer what she could only guess were words of comfort, but she heard only muffled voices, echoes of heartache trying to rephrase the gut-wrenching news. At some point, Kris and Emily left her room and she found herself lying alone in her bed. Her head resting on a pillow wet with tears.

The sleepless night turned into morning and morning into another restless night. It was a relentless merry-go-round of sorrow; her days filled with the mundane and her nights filled with unending worry. Just two days after Lexi had received the news of Ricky's relapse, she got a call from him. He had been honorably released from his service as a full-time missionary. She plainly heard the sadness masked behind the falsetto of lightness he tried to portray. His cancer had come back with a vengeance. He was still in Boston, taking up residence in an ICU unit at Massachusetts General. Rick and Maren had flown out the day after they had learned of his relapse. Once Ricky was a bit more stable, he would be transferred by ambulance to Sloan Kettering Cancer Hospital in New York.

Being diagnosed with cancer was like being told that the monster under your bed was real, and not only were you afraid, but the grown-ups were as well. There is shock. There is pain. There is heartache. And then a numbness encompasses you and you realize that all of the things you thought could never possibly happen to someone you love are now going to happen to you. The numbness begins to subside, and you learn to find peace. You learn to find strength. You learn to fully see the world in a way you had never thought possible. You experience indescribable agony in every aspect of your life. If you survive, you are congratulated and soon forgotten. If you die, you live on forever as a legend. Once you become cancer free, you feel as if you've conquered an unconquerable demon. You have officially made it. You have won. You learn to live with the consequences of treatment and rebuild your life from the wreckage caused by the battle between you and the monster you never wanted to believe existed.

Ricky now stood face to face with that demon, his nightmares coming to life as he came to grips with the cold truth that he would have to once again go into battle. Getting released from his mission was harder than he could put into words. It felt as if he had let everyone around him down somehow but there was nothing he could do to make it right. He missed his mission. He missed the people. He missed the promise of a life he was planning on living after he was home. He missed having a choice in what came next.

Ricky was trying to be brave, but there was an underlying current in his voice that Lexi heard from across the country. The deep ache in her bones, that had begun the day she'd learned of Ricky's relapse, had turned from a slow and steady drip of unease to a constant rush of hurt that coursed through her soul as she found herself questioning the timing of Ricky's relapse. Ricky would do God's will, he would keep his faith and "fight a good fight," of this Lexi was certain. But, the thought of what the fight would cost him, the sacrifices he would make, the price he would pay just to survive, was suffocating.

Lexi had never doubted the reasoning for her own cancer diagnosis, and oddly enough even found that she was grateful for the knowledge and the growth she'd experienced as a result of her journey. She could've done without the nausea and physical pain—but regardless, she was grateful. But Ricky relapsing now just seemed senseless. Her heart hurt for him and the dreaded battle she knew all too well may lie before him. It wasn't just the prospect of Ricky beating cancer that troubled Lexi, it was the lasting effects it could hold for his future—the things that treatment could permanently rip from him, the things it had already stolen from her. A shiver ran up her spine as her mind began its assault of the horrors she'd experienced during the previous two years. Tears spilled over her clear eyes as she bowed her head, unable to keep the terrors that plagued her dreams at bay. She could still recall the feeling of dancing freely for hours on end, hiking with her family without fear of tiring or not being able to breathe, and the thrill of landing her aerial for the first time, and then a hundred times more. All memories of a life she had, a life her mortal body would never allow her to return to. Dreams she once worked so hard for were now reserved for another lifetime. The thought of Ricky enduring this same fate felt like more than her heart could take.

Ricky was finally well enough to be transferred for further treatment. He said goodbye to the local ward members and friends who had come to see him off. The nurses prepared him for transport by strapping his tall frame to a gurney. Well, they said it was a gurney, but to Ricky it felt more like a slab of concrete. As they drove, Ricky talked excitedly of the memories and the friends he had made during his time in Boston. He told his parents of the families on his mission and did his best to remain upbeat and positive, but just as the cancer had found its way back into his bloodstream, the sadness he was fighting to keep at bay found its way back into his heart.

Ricky talked the driver of the ambulance into stopping by the asphalt courts that he had spent so many hours playing streetball at. The old school blacktop courts were as rundown as he remembered, but his heart yearned to play there just one more time. He thought back to the moments that he had played in front of whatever group had gathered there that day. He thought of the times he felt fearless and strong, like he was completely unstoppable. Those times had retired with his black name tag. He was now just another kid with cancer, strapped to a hard bed with tubes running in and out of his ever-weakening body.

The ambulance was sailing along nicely on the freeway. The EMTs had turned the long journey into a party by cranking up the radio. Ricky didn't have to be asked to join the impromptu concert. A distraction was exactly what his heart needed right now. The novelty of the expedition wore off after the first hour, leaving Ricky alone with his thoughts for the remainder of his trip. The humming of the pump that was sending fluids directly into Ricky's body served as the white noise interference he needed. He closed his eyes and began to pray fiercely about the internal war he was facing, but to no avail.

Ricky and his parents had finally made it to the hospital only to find themselves occupying the waiting room of the ICU. Ricky closed his eyes and listened as the hospital buzzed around him. He opened his eyes slowly and looked at his parents, the evidence of the red-eye flight evident on both of their faces. He had been transferred from the metal plank of the ambulance stretcher to a slightly less torturous hospital bed. The top section of his bed had been propped up by the EMT so that Ricky's back had the support of the bed behind it. He watched other patients with curiosity as their beds wheeled past him, an entourage of machines and nurses following closely in their wake. The EMT that had doubled as the DJ on his recent road trip caught the attention of a nurse passing by.

"Hey, can you help us out?" the EMT said while gesturing to Ricky. "I've got a transplant from Boston. The kid relapsed with cancer and he needs a room. Where should I take him?" The nurse exhaled and Ricky guessed it was nearing the end of a long shift for her. She peered around the EMT and glanced at Ricky to determine the intensity of his ailment. He smiled out of habit and that was all the evidence she needed to classify him.

"He looks stable. Give me a few minutes to look at his chart and then we will see where they want to put him. In the meantime, you can wheel him into a room over here so that he's out of the way." She gestured to a makeshift room whose walls consisted of hanging curtains. The nurse promptly walked away with purpose, clearly in a hurry to finish whatever she was doing before being interrupted by the EMT. Maren, Rick, and the EMT were left at Ricky's bedside in the hall. If he were back home there wouldn't be a question—he would go straight to Primary Children's for treatment and have the same doctor and nurses he was used to. He would also have his family and Lex there. But for now, he just had to lay on a plastic slab while they tried to figure out what to do with him.

Ricky turned to see a set of swinging doors open to reveal a young man that looked to be just a little younger than himself. He stood about 5'7" and his ebony skin held the jaundice of a liver that was not functioning correctly. The young man walked with the collected confidence of a hospital frequent flier. He was accompanied by a woman who bore a striking resemblance to the young man. The two of them were clearly comfortable in these halls. As the young man neared Ricky, he smiled.

"Hey man, how are you doin'?"

"I'm good, just waiting to see where they are going to put me," Ricky responded.

"I have been there before," the young man said as he laughed with ease. "They never quite know what to do with me."

"You come here a lot?" Ricky asked.

"Off and on pretty much for the past five years," the young man said. "My name is Moses and this is my mom, Deborah," he added. The woman at his side smiled warmly and extended her hand. Ricky took it easily and introduced himself and his parents.

"Come find us when you get settled and let us know where y'all end up," said Deborah. "We're just heading up to the teen room. You guys should come check it out when you get a chance." They each said their goodbyes and Moses and Deborah continued on their inpatient journey.

After what seemed like an eternity, the nurse approached Ricky and his parents once again. The decision had been made to send him to the ICU. It could have been the fact that they didn't have beds available anywhere else. It was more likely the fact that Ricky's white blood cell count was over 186,000 as opposed to the normal count of 4,500 to 11,000. Whatever the case, he was grateful to be getting out of the lobby. He was not a fan of being on display for the whole of the hospital crowd.

Ricky ran his hand through his thick, dark hair out of habit. The chestnut locks that belonged to remission would be gone soon, just like his strength. If this relapse was anything like his original diagnosis, his consolation for losing his physical traits would be a moon-shaped face brought on by steroids, and never-ending nausea with a side of mouth sores. He was the cancer kid, again. He was slowly coming to terms with what that meant. His future could no longer hold the dreams that got him through his first battle. But this time he had more to lose. Had cancer, the very thing that brought Lexi into his life, somehow cost him the blessing of marrying her? Ricky knew that Lexi was not as healthy as she was before treatment, but overall she was consistently getting stronger. He, on the other hand, was headed in the opposite direction. Would his diagnosis be the thing that drove them apart? The thought was too much to bear. He was meant to marry Lexi, he had to. He had been praying about it for months now. Cancer had brought them together, but over the last few years he had fallen in love with every part of Lexi. He knew in his heart that a connection like theirs was a once in eternity occurrence.

Lexi continued praying for Ricky, as she always had. But somehow these prayers felt as if they were filled with more purpose, more intent. She needed understanding. How could she help him wade through these rough waters when she felt as if she were drowning? She needed a lifeline. Now was not the time to turn away from God, but towards Him. She knew she couldn't make it through this without His help. She prayed. She pleaded. She listened. And then she prayed some more. She needed God to be with her, to clear her mind from the ugliness of reality and fill it with the perfect beauty of eternity.

Over the coming days, the peace that Lexi's soul had so desperately been craving began to slowly break through her sorrow. She began to understand that this trial was not meant to punish Ricky or take anything from him any more than her cancer was meant to punish her. On the contrary, Lexi was strongly reminded that trials were given to help a person grow and become who God would have them be. She didn't need to fully understand the timing or know each aspect of God's plan to have faith and know that He was watching out for Ricky. She knew He was. She could feel it. God was not focused on Ricky's physical attributes or making sure that crowds of people knew his name. None of that had eternal merit. The perfect love that God had for Ricky filled Lexi's being. She saw her best friend in a whole new light. She saw his flaws and imperfections and then saw everything that he could be. She saw Ricky the way that she knew

God saw him. She fervently prayed that this beautiful love and knowledge would fill Ricky's heart too.

Thinking of Ricky brought a smile to her face, as it always did. She thought of his willingness to go and do whatever God would have him do. She thought of the opportunity he had been given to play on an elite AAU team in Las Vegas with the promise of receiving offers of playing at the next level if he would just put his mission off a little longer, but he chose to put God first. The peace that she had been craving for the past several days encompassed Lexi like the warm blankets they used to give her at the hospital. She knew things were going to get worse before they got better, but she felt comfort nonetheless.

The long hospital days turned into long hospital nights. Ricky spent the hours walking the hospital floor, meeting new friends, and texting Lexi or sending her funny videos to make her laugh. Each interaction he had with Lexi only furthered his conviction that they were meant to be together. Yet, he could not shake the nagging thoughts of Lexi moving on with her life and leaving him behind. He began to worry—the kind of worry that sat deep in his gut because he couldn't voice it. His thoughts began to unravel the way a sweater does when a loose string is pulled. *I love Lexi. That doesn't seem like a strong enough word. Everyone loves Lexi. I am IN LOVE with Lexi. I want to be with her forever and always have her near me. I can't make it through this life without her by my side. She knows parts of me that no one else does. She brings out parts of me that no one else can.* Ricky had opened his heart to Lexi in ways he had never allowed himself to do with anyone. Of course they had talked about cancer—the ugliness of living in a world that most are completely naive too. Cancer had overwhelming lasting effects, most of which Ricky worked hard to ignore, but with Lexi he did not have to shut that part of himself off, he didn't have to hide anything. They spoke about fears he didn't dare voice to others. But it was more than that. Ricky had shared his childhood with Lexi. He spoke openly about the memories that made him laugh, the memories that made him cry, and all of the memories in between. Lexi had seen every piece of Ricky and somehow still loved him.

Ricky knew that Lexi was destined for great things, but would her plans include him? He felt sick, and it had nothing to do with the chemo. Nothing brought him more comfort than the thought of Lexi by his side. She was his safe space. But somehow this blessing seemed as if it were reserved for another life, one that didn't involve a relapse. How could he possibly ask Lexi to be his wife, let alone his girlfriend, with a road of treatment ahead of him? Lexi knew better than anyone what cancer treatment looked like. She was done with it and was moving forward with her life. She had been accepted to college and had started making plans for nursing school. Surely, she wouldn't willingly dive back into this world. Lexi knew better than anyone what cancer treatment looked like. She understood the side effects that came with it. Surely, she would not want to dive back into a world that she had barely escaped. The alternative thought sent sharp pains through his chest. *What if she chooses to continue forward with her life and continue to date other people? How am I supposed to marry someone else when I know I can never care for someone the way I care for her?* Ricky's heart was set on Lexi, and he knew no one would take her place. But, could someone else take his place?

For the next few weeks Ricky did his best to suppress the frustration he found himself experiencing. Why would God give him such a strong impression only to take it away? He silently wrestled with emotions he did not want to have. He did his best to occupy his time by willing himself to stay happy and go out of his way to show love to others, while simultaneously hiding the thoughts and struggles he was facing on the inside. Distraction was his game plan. It always had been. Why should he feel hard emotions when he could push them aside and carry on as if they didn't exist? Ricky couldn't be the sad cancer kid. He couldn't let those hard emotions in. What if they never left? Emotions were not part of the Stafford game plan. They were hard and messy and uncomfortable. Why should he have to start feeling them now?

Ricky returned to trying to distract himself and Maren with his ukulele. Heartache rose and he pushed it down. Sadness bubbled up and he compressed it. Fear surfaced and he compacted it. Rick had left the day before to return home. Ricky tried to wrap his head around the fact that he would likely be here for a while. The seriousness of his condition had not yet fully hit him, but he did understand enough to know that they did not drive you over 200 miles in an ambulance just to release you the next day. Ricky's shoulders slumped as the weight of his situation settled. Hospital life was never fun, hospital life away from friends and family was just plain rough.

"He won't be able to come home until after Christmas," Lexi said. She had just gotten home from school and went straight to the fridge to look for the high calorie foods she had to eat every couple of hours. It wasn't the typical diet for a teenage girl, but she wasn't exactly a typical teenage girl. Thanks to cancer, her body no longer processed any food on its own. So, she would spend the rest of her life taking three enzyme pills before she ate anything and three pills after to help her body process the nutrition she gave it. She'd then pray that the food, and the enzymes, would stay in her stomach long enough to be digested. It was an exhausting process, but one that was necessary to keep herself from losing any more weight.

"I shouldn't complain because we text throughout the day and we FaceTime or Marco Polo every night, but it's just not the same. I wish I could be there for him," Lexi said as she spread the extra mayo on two thick slices of bread. "I just feel like I need to be with him. I need to see him in person to make sure he's okay and to let him know he's not alone." She added mustard, turkey, and avocado to complete her sandwich and sat down at the table in hopes she could distract her stomach from the nausea that always accompanied food. Chemo ruining food for her might have been harder to take than being bald. She exhaled and prepared herself to take a dutiful bite.

Just then a slow smile crept across Emily's lips as if she just realized she was holding the key to unlock the world's happiness. Emily's emerald eyes danced with excitement as she turned to look at Lexi directly.

"I just thought of something," said Emily. The moment was contagious to watch, and Lexi couldn't help but laugh a little at how excited her mom got when she came up with an idea. Lex subconsciously took another obligatory bite as she anxiously waited to see what Emily had come up with to raise her spirits this time.

"Lex, Grandma works for an airline. Maybe we can see if she has buddy passes and we could surprise Ricky in New York."

A glimmer of hope crossed Lexi's blue eyes. "Really?" Lexi said, swallowing quickly. Big mistake—the trick to keeping food in her stomach these days was small bites, slow eating, high calories. Eating was nothing more than a job for Lexi and she was working on getting it down to a science. She quickly took a few breaths to calm her stomach and allow her gag reflex to reset.

"Yeah!" Emily said. "I fly for free so we would only need a pass for you. We could leave on Saturday night after your drill competition and I would fly back Sunday night. I'll call Grandma and then text Maren to see what she thinks about it."

By the end of the day the plan was in full action. With the help of Lexi's grandma, Lexi and Emily would be flying to New York to surprise Ricky within a week.

Throughout the coming days Ricky was surprised and grateful to get visits not just from local church members and people he had served with in his mission, but also from Moses and Deborah. Moses had spent the last four years going from being diagnosed with one rare disease after another. Rosai Dorfman's disease had hit him first in 2014. In 2016 he was diagnosed with Langerhans cell histiocytosis. This was followed up with Hodgkin's Lymphoma in 2016. The young man was a walking anomaly.

When Ricky was finally well enough to leave the ICU, Moses and Deborah gave Ricky and Maren a tour of the famous "teen room." The room was open and inviting. It contained multiple gaming stations and a few tables where people could gather around and play cards or board games. The setup and design of the room gave the blue walls a resemblance akin to open fields as opposed to city limits.

The days were like a bad oxymoron that seemed to drag on and simultaneously fly by. Before Lexi knew it, they were on a plane to New York to see Ricky for the first time in eight months. Lexi let her head tiredly fall against the small airplane window as she looked out and watched the lights of the city fade below the clouds. She knew she should try to sleep, but sleep wasn't something that would come tonight. She had too many thoughts in her head, too much to understand. In a few hours she would be going to visit Ricky in the hospital.

Over the past few years Lexi had met a lot of kids with cancer and had the chance to become good friends with many of them. The majority of her cancer friends were much younger than she was, but she had been fortunate enough to develop a few close relationships with other teenagers that also resided in the cancer world. Being a teenager is hard enough. Being a teenager with cancer is brutal. You have no privacy, no social life, and are trying to navigate figuring out who you are amongst an onslaught of normal hormones that are constantly being altered and angered by a barrage of medications. The journey was nearly impossible.

Despite the age of her friends, Lexi would often go visit them in the hospital and they would come to visit her. There was a kinship in the cancer world. It was the club no one wanted to join, but once you were in, you were accepted fully. No one cared about who you were before you got diagnosed or where you lived. No one cared about the clothes you wore or what kind of house your family lived in. Cancer was the great equalizer. It stripped away everything about a person except the very purest parts of them. There were no expectations or pretenses, just love and patience. Everybody looked after everyone else because they were all just doing their best to survive, quite literally.

But this wasn't just any friend that Lexi was going to visit, this was Ricky. The word "friend" didn't seem sufficient for the connection they shared. From the first time they'd met Lexi had felt an unknown force pull her towards Ricky. At first she counted it as nothing more than cancer being their common thread, and age strengthening that bond. But, with increased hospital stays, she had the chance to meet other cancer patients. Lexi found that teenage cancer patients often migrated to one another, as they were considered more of a rarity.

Lexi had met her best friend, Ashtyn, just shortly after Lexi was diagnosed. Ashtyn had UML, unidentified myeloid leukemia. She was in remission the first time that Lexi had met her, but she relapsed shortly after. Once again, Ash had beat the rare cancer and was currently in remission. The two of them had become fast friends, and as time went on, their bond was solidified. The girls spent ice cream nights giggling about boys and shedding tears over cancer.

"Lex, why don't you date Ricky?" Ash had asked during one of their late-night talks.

"We have gone on a couple of dates," Lexi answered simply, knowing full well that this was not what Ash was referring to. Ash raised her penciled-in eyebrows and approached the topic again, more directly.

"C'mon, Lex, you know what I mean. He is cute and you guys clearly have a connection."

"It's Ricky, he has a connection with everyone," Lex said with a slight tilt of her head. "He's cute, but we are just friends. That boy needs a mission." Ash smiled and raised her faux eyebrows up and down as she patiently waited for an explanation, so Lexi continued, "Ricky is a great person and he has a lot of really great qualities . . ."

"But . . ." Ash said, her patience beginning to falter. Life was short; she had found that a direct approach produced faster results.

"But, it's just not our time yet," Lexi said as she lifted her shoulders and let them fall.

Lexi recalled the fond memory in a new light. She thought back to the way that her relationship with Ricky had changed. She realized that with every visit, every text, and every email, she and Ricky had grown closer. Despite her desire to protect her heart, he had somehow woven himself into the fabric of her life. The realization was both comforting and unsettling to Lexi as she stared out the small window of the plane, praying that the night sky would absorb her thoughts and let her drift to sleep.

"Are you doing okay?" Emily asked as she shifted in her seat.

"Yeah, I'm good," Lexi said as she gave her mom a small smile. She watched as Emily settled back into her airplane seat that doubled as her bed for the night, and then allowed her mind to return to Ricky and the cloud of emotions that now surrounded him. Ricky and Lexi had been best friends when he left on his mission. She had openly told him about the boys she had dated and what traits they had that she did or did not like. He had done the same in return. They had been on dates together, and group dates with others. They had talked about their past and dreamt about their future. Cancer may have been the starting point of their relationship, but it was now just a small piece of the puzzle they had constructed together. It was clear that something had changed over the past eight months. Every email they'd exchanged brought them closer, despite the fact that they were thousands of miles apart. Friends, family, and even nurses commented on their undeniable connection. She wasn't sure exactly what it was, but something about Ricky made her completely at ease in a way that almost scared her. She wasn't used to feeling a bond so strong to someone and, until this point, she had been able to use time as a safeguard.

Then, Ricky left on his mission. With every email she felt him grow spiritually stronger and their connection undeniably deepened. He shared with her not only the successes that came as a result of his efforts, but his worries and frustrations as well. He allowed himself to open up to her in a way that he had never done with anyone before. She found herself doing the same. Just as sure as her ragged lungs breathed in the oxygen needed to keep her alive, she knew in the framework of her brittle bones that Ricky Stafford would always play a part in her life. The plane began its descent. Lexi's breath caught as the reality that neither miles nor a mission would be standing between them any longer.

Whether it was lack of sleep or the nerves of seeing Ricky in person after eight months of being apart, Lexi's heart was beating so hard as she exited the plane that she thought it might be visible to the other passengers. A sudden feeling of unease entered her thoughts as she mindlessly followed Emily off the plane. But, Maren had assured Lexi that having her around was sure to strengthen Ricky's heart. Lexi held to that reassurance as a lifeline as she took another breath and found the closest family restroom. After flying most of the night Lexi hurried to make herself somewhat presentable in the small airport bathroom while Emily called for an uber to take them to the hospital. This was not exactly how Lexi pictured her first trip to New York, but then again, she never pictured Ricky relapsing on his mission either.

"Hey you two!" Maren said from the top of the hospital escalator.

Lexi looked up and smiled, still trying to calm her chemo-ridden heart and crude lungs from the excitement that continued to pile on. Lexi's small nose still sported a touch of pink as her body worked to return feeling to her extremities. Utah winters were notorious for the best snow on earth, but they paled in comparison to the bitter sting of a New York frost.

"Hey!" Emily responded. "How have you been?"

"Oh, you know—just trying to not be too bored in the hospital," Maren said with an easy laugh.

She hugged each of them quickly as they got to the top of the escalator and started walking down the hall to the waiting room. It was still early in the morning and most of the patients were either asleep or not feeling up to venturing out of their rooms just yet. As the three of them passed the nurses' station, Maren introduced Lexi and Emily to the nurses sitting at the desk. It was clear that the Staffords had already made themselves at home at Memorial Sloan Kettering Cancer Hospital. The trio continued down the hall until reaching a wide-open room.

"Hang tight and I'll go wake his lazy bum up and get him out of bed," Maren said.

As Maren walked down the hall, Emily looked around the comfortable room. It had been furnished with a few couches and a couple of matching chairs as their companions. This space was set to accommodate large family visits but was not so big as to be overwhelming for smaller group settings as well. Emily smiled subconsciously as she couldn't help but notice that the color scheme seemed to match that of Primary Children's Hospital. *Either they are banking on the fact that these really are calming colors, or all hospitals have the same interior decorator,* Emily thought to herself. She took a glance over at Lexi and realized that she was pacing from one chair to the next. Lexi unwillingly made the decision between the two chairs and sat down. Precisely 3.33 seconds later she began shifting in her seat.

"Can't get comfortable?" Emily asked with a grin, knowing full well that it was the nerves and not the furniture that was causing Lexi's inability to hold still.

"I'm just not sure where to sit," Lexi said looking a little distraught. "I was going to sit there but then he could see me coming from down the hall and I wanted it to be a surprise. Then I was thinking of sitting here but I'm not sure what to do with my hands," Lexi said as she held her traitorous hands up and looked at them in irritation. They had clearly betrayed her by not knowing what to do with themselves.

"I think where you are sitting is gre . . ." Emily began but before she could finish, Lexi's nerves continued their ramble.

"What should I say?" Lexi blurted out looking completely at a loss. She paused for a moment to remind herself to breathe and Emily took the risk of beginning again.

"First, you should switch to decaf," Emily replied solemnly to elicit a laugh from Lexi. The muscles in Lexi's face relaxed slightly and she was able to momentarily push aside the anxiety tying knots in her stomach. Emily continued, "I think the chair that you're sitting in is great and I think that he is going to be so excited to see you that you can say whatever comes to your mind or nothing at all. He's just going to be so happy that you're here."

"I don't know why I'm so nervous," Lexi said as she exhaled a breath that she didn't realize she was holding.

"There is nothing to be nervous about honey," Emily said. "It's Ricky."

"I know, but it feels different this time. How's my hair?"

"It's beautiful, sis," Emily assured her.

"I guess it doesn't really matter," Lexi added with a small laugh. "He's seen me with no hair."

"And no eyelashes," Emily added factually.

Lexi nodded her head in agreement and waited anxiously, wondering exactly how far away Ricky's hospital room actually was.

"Ricky, get up," said Maren. "There is a kid in the family room up here who is really struggling and I think you could help."

Sleepily, Ricky rubbed his cheeks, blew out his breath and ran his hands through his dark hair. He knew better than to argue with his mom when she had an idea. He did his best to paint a smile on his face and slipped on his unlaced Nikes. Tying shoes was no longer worth the energy it required. His tall frame sauntered lazily down the hall. He prayed that his unyielding discouragement as of late might be cloaked by the sleepiness that was evident on his face. The stillness of the morning hospital proved to be the perfect incubator for the thoughts Ricky had been battling the past few weeks. The spiritual barrage from the day before continued on, unimpeded. Ricky fell into step beside Maren, and they walked the long corridor to the family room. Each patient door an unlikely, yet unwavering soldier guarding its inhabitants religiously. With every step he was assaulted with worries, fears, and doubts. Ricky's mind was too tired to muster a distraction right now. As a result, the emotions he had been fighting to keep restricted broke free. What was he doing here? Why now? What more was there to learn? What else would he lose?

Ricky was supposed to be on his mission, getting stronger, and emailing Lexi. He was supposed to be released in sixteen months from now and be greeted by his family and friends at the airport. Lexi would be there too, of course, and as he was coming down the escalator to the many cheers, he would look right at Lexi and wink. She would smile a smile that was meant only for him. His stomach would fill with the nervous excitement that only she could instill in him, and they would share a moment in the midst of the chaos without anyone ever realizing it happened. He would ask her to go on a date with him the very next day, and the day after that, and the day after that.

But there would be no completion of his mission, no getting stronger, no grand homecoming, no wink, no special moment. There was just a random kid in the hospital waiting room who needed a friend. So, Ricky did his best to find his smile and prepared to be that friend.

As he neared the waiting room, Ricky worked to refocus his thoughts. His shoulders slouched, bearing the full weight of his emotions. He could not muster the strength necessary to lift them. Instead, he rolled them back, hoping to appear less downtrodden. Ricky exhaled as he approached the room and squared his shoulders. He looked for a smile, but those were becoming harder to come by these days. He did his best to force the corners of his mouth upwards. Ricky had just passed the threshold of the waiting room door when his eyes caught sight of a face he knew all too well, a face that had hung on the wall of his missionary apartment, the face of his best friend.

His breath caught as her clear blue eyes met his from across the room. He looked from Lexi back to Maren. Was this really happening? Could she really be here? The conspiratorial grin on Maren's face confirmed that she had been in on this plan from the beginning. Ricky quickly looked back to Lexi and saw the smile that was playing across her lips.

"Fancy meeting you here," Lexi said, her blue eyes dancing brighter than he had ever remembered.

Ricky stood dumbfounded as Lexi began to walk towards him. He swallowed hard. He looked from Lexi to Maren and back to Lexi again as he willed his bottom lip to still from the raw emotion that was causing it to shake. At that moment Ricky's untethered feelings took over as he took a step towards Lexi and enveloped her in his waiting arms. His prayers had been answered, his dream a reality. Lexi was here, against all unlikely odds, in the hospital with him in New York. He did his best to fight back tears as fears of the past few weeks seemed to dissipate in her presence. He held her, not wanting to ever let go. In that moment, all of his frustrations, disappointments, and discouragements were replaced with Lexi's love.

But it was more than Lexi's love that Ricky felt. The perfect love of God surrounded him as surely as his arms surrounded Lexi. All of Ricky's worries, doubts, and fears left his heart. He knew of a surety that God was not only aware of him, but of his individual happiness. All of his prayers had been heard and somehow he was now holding the answer in his arms. Ricky now understood that the resolutions to his problems hadn't come before because he was still learning to trust God and His timing; to have complete faith in His plan. In that moment, there was no question in Ricky's mind that God's timing was perfect. His plan was perfect.

Ricky and Lexi embraced one another and held on as if nothing else in the world mattered, because in that moment it didn't. They were together and that was everything. All of the time spent apart, the emails, the late-night phone calls, the unspoken emotions, all of it came to the surface and spilled down Ricky's cheeks. Everything was felt but nothing needed to be said as they stood in the doorway of a hospital visiting area and held each other. Ricky's chin rested perfectly on top of Lexi's head, as if their bodies were designed to compliment one another. They were thousands of miles from where they grew up, but both of them realized in that moment that they were finally home.

Chapter 12

"I fell in love the way you fall asleep: slowly, and then all at once." —John Green

Ricky had always planned to date Lexi when he got home from his mission, walking the halls of the hospital and having his mom chaperone was never part of the plan. He was quickly learning that his plans for the future were as solid as a house built upon the sand and his ability to adapt to the tides of life were pertinent to his survival.

Lexi was here now, in New York with him and he was no longer a missionary. She somehow seemed more beautiful than he remembered—even more beautiful than her pictures that he had moved from his planner to the wall of his missionary apartment. They comfortably strolled the halls of the hospital. Ricky beamed and Lexi blushed each time a nurse met Lexi and remarked, "Oh, this is the Lexi we've heard so much about!" Ricky watched in awe as within minutes of being introduced, Lexi was talking with the nurse like an old friend. Ricky and Lexi continued down the hall laughing and joking as if they had never left one another's side.

They returned from their walk. Ricky's body felt the physical exertion he had spent on the outing. However, he knew that his racing heart could not solely be attributed to the return of the cancer. Ricky climbed into the hospital bed. He raised the top half of it so that the bed more closely resembled a couch, as opposed to an uncomfortable plastic contraption that he was expected to sleep in.

"Wanna watch a movie?" Ricky said, as he patted the spot next to him. Lexi sat down and the familiar plastic pad crinkled beneath them as it had each time she sat on her hospital bed in Primary Children's. Her heart began to flutter but the chemo-induced arrhythmia was not the culprit. The pull she felt towards Ricky was palpable, the electricity tangible. They had watched countless movies side by side in and out of the hospital, but there was always a reason they couldn't be more than just friends. Those reasons had vanished as quickly as Lexi's eyelashes after transplant.

Lexi exhaled silently and willed her heart to slow before it beat completely out of her chest. She focused on the rise and fall of her lungs. She was terrible at flirting, she knew it. Ricky knew it. What she was about to do couldn't actually be considered flirting, but it was as close as her nerves would let her get today. Lexi slowly laid her head on Ricky's shoulder and pretended as if she were asleep, a simple gesture but one that took all of her courage. She could feel the soft flutter of her lashes humming with excitement against her cheek. Things felt different for her now; being with Ricky felt different.

Ricky's grin grew so big it was almost painful. He hoped the pounding in his chest wouldn't disrupt Lexi as she did her best to feign exhaustion on his shoulder. Her dark lashes twitched as rapidly as her muscles had during treatment. She was working so hard to give the illusion that she was sleeping that Ricky had to stifle a laugh. She really was the worst at flirting, but he didn't mind the attempt. A few minutes later the nurse entered the room to take Ricky's vitals. She attached the black adult-sized cuff to Ricky's bicep and pushed the button on the portable blood pressure machine. The cuff began to tighten against his arm but Ricky paid no mind to it. His focus was on the way that one of Lexi's short brown curls had fallen forward. It had come to rest just below her real eyebrow. Ricky fought the urge to try to brush it back, not fully trusting himself to touch her face without waking her from her counterfeit catnap.

"Hmm," the nurse said. "It looks like your heart rate is higher than normal."

Ricky blushed unashamed as Maren responded. "Yeah, I'm betting it won't come down until she lifts her head off of his shoulder either," she said, as she motioned to Lexi with a nod of her head.

Ricky just smiled sweetly and looked down at Lex, fully aware that she was not actually asleep, but grateful that she continued her charade. Ricky's eyes took in Lexi's chestnut curls that now generously covered the bald head she had when they had first met. He noticed the ebony lashes that lay so softly against her porcelain skin, the freckles that sprinkled her delicate nose. He saw the corner of her mouth turn up ever so slightly and then return to its "sleeping position." His mind flooded with pictures and possibilities of the life he could build with Lexi by his side. Ricky knew that he couldn't let Lexi leave New York without telling her how he felt. Her presence made him feel invincible. With her hand in his, it didn't matter what life held, he would come off conqueror. The strength she emanated was tangible and Ricky knew that there was nothing he couldn't do with her by his side.

The day had been spent next to Ricky's side and Lexi had loved every minute of it. Her body was physically exhausted from flying all night but her mind and heart were still racing from the confession that Ricky had shared with her that day. His words circled around her mind like a merry-go-round she never wanted to step away from.

"So what do you think about all of this, Lex?" Maren asked Lexi as the two of them walked briskly through the chill of Central Park as quickly as Lexi's body would allow them to move. They were heading to the apartment that had served as temporary residence to Maren. Lexi could feel the cold December air nipping her nose, but the adrenaline rush from Ricky's earlier emotional outpouring had sent her blood racing through her limbs in such a way that she doubted that she would ever again feel cold.

"What do I think about what?" Lexi asked casually.

She knew exactly what Maren was referring to but wanted a couple of minutes to try to gather her thoughts before the conversation switched from the small talk they had been sharing to the more personal turn she knew it was about to take.

"I might have gotten back from my walk a little sooner than I let on. I heard you guys talking and wanted to know what was going on, so I listened in. I heard Ricky finally told you how he feels about you. What do you think about all of that?"

Lex exhaled to buy herself a little more time. "He's my best friend," she said, instinctively using the same line she had a hundred times before when someone asked why they weren't dating.

"But . . .?" Maren asked. They had made it through the frigid winds of Central Park and had arrived at the apartment building. Lexi felt her nose begin to defrost as the warmth of the regulated temperature permeated through her scarf. She swallowed and, before she knew it, her fears were spilling out freely.

"But maybe it's just that I'm the first girl that he has seen or got to spend time with in over eight months, or maybe it's because he's sick again and he knows that I understand what it's like and he needs someone there. I mean, I'd be there anyway because no one should have to go through cancer alone. I'm just not really sure what to make of all of it. I don't want to risk losing my best friend if things don't work out."

Lexi's heart was the only thing left untouched by her wretched, cancerous disease, the only piece of her left unscathed. This wasn't by coincidence but design. Lexi knew she must protect it, and others from fully seeing it. Surely, people could not see the reality of the life she lived. If they did, they would leave. Cancer was the club that everyone wanted to admire from afar. No one wanted to buy the membership. Ricky had lived his own journey and been such an important part of hers already. He had seen her at some extremely low points in her journey. Of course, she would be there for him when he needed her, but a healthy relationship could not simply be built on a trauma bond. She loved him too much for that.

Maren looked as if she was listening but had clearly detached herself from the words being spoken. Lexi couldn't help but notice that a slight smile was playing on the corner of Maren's lips.

"Lex, this has nothing to do with him not being able to go on dates for the last eight months and everything to do with how he feels about you."

Lexi looked at her quizzically and Maren continued. "You probably didn't know this, but I have access to Ricky's email account. I log in regularly to see who he is emailing and who is emailing him.

I read the emails people would send him and his response, but for some reason I couldn't read your messages that you sent him, only his responses to you. If I'm being honest, it drove me crazy, only getting half of the conversation," she said with a chuckle before continuing on. "I began to notice how often he was emailing you and how his responses to you were so different than they were to anyone else. I didn't put too much thought into it. A couple of months ago I started bugging Ricky because I had this girl that I wanted him to email. Her mom and I are friends so we had the whole thing planned out. We thought that she and Ricky would be super great together and should start emailing. She was really pretty, tall, athletic, and getting ready to go on a mission. She was the type of girl I always knew Ricky would marry. Her and Ricky would get home around the same time from their missions, so I figured it was perfect.

"I sent Ricky her picture and totally talked her up. She spoke German and I thought that Ricky could impress her with his German speaking skills. After some convincing, Ricky indulged me, kind of. He wrote the most boring email ever to this girl. Honestly, it was pitiful."

"Really?" Lex said with a laugh. "That's crazy. He's so good at talking to new people. He's never shy."

"It wasn't because he's shy. It's because he didn't want to do it and he knew I would keep badgering him until he did. I read the email that he wrote to her and when she didn't write back, I told him it was because his first email was so lame and he needed to write to her again. His second email was worse than the first, if you can believe it."

Lexi let out another small giggle, liking how the story was playing out. Her emails with Ricky were never boring. They talked about everything from the mundane to their wildest dreams and their greatest fears to what made them the happiest.

Maren continued on. "I tried emailing him to encourage him to write her a third email and really put some effort into it this time. I guess he had finally had enough of me bugging him, so rather than write another email to the girl, he sent me an email. He told me, 'Mom, I already know who I am supposed to marry so talking to anyone else is just a waste of time.'"

Lexi's heart skipped a beat at these words, but she wasn't sure if she wanted to hope for the outcome she thought might be next in the story.

"Of course I wanted to know who Ricky thought he was going to marry," Maren said. "So, I asked him and he told me it was you."

Lexi's breath caught.

Maren continued without prompting. "His exact words were, 'I'm gonna marry Lex, Mom. I've known for a while now and ever since I knew for sure that she was the one I wanted to be with forever, it's like I have no desire to really talk to other girls at all. It feels like I am just trying to pass time until I can be with Lex.'"

Lexi was speechless.

"He sent me that email in October, Lex," Maren added. "We talked about it for awhile after that. I told him that your body wasn't super healthy and even if you keep getting stronger you will probably never be as healthy as you were before cancer. He told me he didn't care about that. I even told him that you probably can't have your own kids." Lexi winced slightly as her physical shortcomings were laid out one by one. Maren continued, "He told me that he probably couldn't have kids either and that the two of you could just adopt when you were ready. I really tried to put it all out there, but he just became more firm in his conviction to you. His feelings have nothing to do with him being away from girls for eight months. His feelings have everything to do with him being away from *you* for eight months. You being here now is not a coincidence. He has been struggling so much. He's trying to hide it, but I've never seen him so down. I've noticed such a change in his whole demeanor since you've been here. He is laughing again. You saved him."

"Really?" was the only word that managed to escape Lexi's mouth.

"Yeah," Maren said with a small laugh. "Hey, are you hungry?" Maren asked casually as if she hadn't just turned Lexi's whole world upside down. Together they made a midnight snack and their conversation continued for another two hours before they headed to bed.

Lexi's eyelids grew heavy and she knew she needed to sleep. Her body had provided her with enough strength to make it through the day, and even the bonus strength to walk through Central Park. She knew she could demand no more from it today. She closed her eyes and Ricky's face projected on the back of her lids. She felt the corners of her mouth turn upwards as the conversation they had earlier that day played through her mind.

"Lex, I kinda like you," Ricky whispered as they were watching their movie. His arm was comfortably draped around Lexi's shoulders and her head was resting on his chest. She had long given up her charade of being asleep. Maren had gone to the cafeteria to get some lunch and had likely run into Deborah. Ricky was not about to miss this opportunity that they were finally alone to tell Lexi how he felt.

"Just kinda?" Lexi replied, feigning insult through a sidelong glance. Ricky smiled softly at her teasing but continued on. He had been waiting months, years if he was honest, to tell Lexi what was truly in his heart.

"I really like you, Lex," he said, and without hesitation added, "I love you." Her crystal eyes flitted with surprise but held his gaze.

"In the gross way?" she asked with a soft smile.

"Definitely," he said with a smile of his own.

Lexi felt her cheeks flush at the recollection of Ricky's lips on hers for the first time. She replayed the scene over and over. It had quickly become her favorite love story. Her body may be completely worn out, but her heart was alive and beating fine.

The following day Ricky couldn't believe he was walking through the halls of Sloan Kettering Hospital holding the hand of the most amazing person he had ever met. He ventured a long glance at her as she was asking the nurse about how her day was going. He noticed the way that the nurse so comfortably conversed with Lexi, as if they were lifelong friends. He noticed the way that Lexi's presence helped everyone around her to feel at ease. This girl would change the world, and he would be holding her hand while she did it. Lexi turned her head slightly and realized that Ricky was watching her. He smiled her favorite smile, and she wondered what he could be thinking about that made him so happy.

They walked into the teen room hand in hand and found Moses and Deborah already taking up residence at one of the tables. Ricky had hung out with the pair multiple times since coming to Sloan Kettering. He shared stories of his mission and his life back home. He never failed to share stories of Lexi, as well. Ricky and Lexi walked towards Moses and Deborah. Deborah's smile widely broadened with excitement. One had to only be around her for a short while before recognizing that Moses's optimism and love of life was an inherited trait.

"Hey guys, this is Lexi, my best friend that I told you about," Ricky said.

Deborah wasted no time walking over to Lexi and enveloping her in a genuine hug. Lexi's heart absorbed the love that Deborah so freely gave and returned the embrace.

Moses looked at Lexi then at Ricky. He noticed the way that their fingers were entwined. He raised the bare skin where his eyebrows should have been and smiled at Ricky. "Best friend, huh? Doesn't look like just a best friend," he said with an easy laugh and added, "Hey Lex, it's nice to finally meet you. Ricky won't shut up about you." The group passed the afternoon carelessly with a variety of board games, laughter, and friendship.

Lexi made it through security and waited in the terminal of the JFK airport for her plane to board. Her body had long since given up trying to keep pace with her heart. She melted exhaustedly into a chair. Her bags fell carelessly into the seat beside her. Her phone buzzed in her hand and she looked down to see a text from Emily. Emily had left within hours of arriving, but Lexi had chosen to stay in New York with Ricky for a few extra days. Those days had been filled with everything from hours of endless conversation, to medication, to sweet stolen kisses when no one was watching. Ricky had been discharged the day before and given the okay to stay in the small apartment that had become Maren's temporary home. The day had been spent exploring New York hand in hand and talking to the insurance company to get at home prescriptions filled. Ricky found his temper bubbling up at the frustration with the latter, but Lexi's calm demeanor put his soul at ease and spared the insurance rep from the string of profanities that generally accompanied his frustrations. Lexi smiled at the memory of the last few days and all of the possibilities that her future with Ricky could hold. Her phone buzzed again, reminding her of Emily's text.

"Just wanted to see if you made it to the airport okay. Can't wait to hear all about your trip!"

Lexi smiled and confirmed that she had arrived at the airport safely. As for her trip, she wasn't quite sure where to begin. She had texted Emily throughout each day and tried to catch her up with what had taken place through a quick call at night, but it seemed as if it would take an entire lifetime to fully process everything that had happened during her short visit to New York. The thought of Ricky caused a rush of complicated emotions to stir within Lexi's heart that left her feeling excited, dizzy, scared, and a little unsure. She was young but her heart had felt love before and lost it. What she had with Ricky was new and thrilling, yet it brought her strength and peace. It calmed her fears just to be near him. She leaned on him far more than she'd ever planned to and enjoyed him in her life more than she had allowed herself to admit.

"I'm going to need a solid week of best friend-mode conversation to catch you up on everything, Momma."

Lexi hit send on her phone just as the stewardess called for her flight to board.

The plane landed in Salt Lake City and Ricky could feel his heart relax. His body, on the other hand, was tight and uncomfortable as a result of the steroids he was taking and the treatment-induced diabetes that was beginning to set in. But, that didn't matter now. He was finally home. After spending over a month in New York, and missing the traditional Christmas and New Years Eve festivities, Ricky was finally home. Crowds of people scurried about in an effort to make flights, meet up with loved ones, or find a quick bite to eat before their aircraft departed.

Ricky took a moment to breathe strength into his limbs. He checked his carryon to be certain that the hand-carved jewelry box he had found for Lexi had made the trip unscathed. He opened it to reveal the delicate necklace he had bought for her. She would love the simple gold chain and the delicate letter "A" that hung from it. He thought of the moment he would be able to put it around her neck and clasp it in place for her and then hold her in his arms once more. He made sure his uke was secured to his backpack, tightened the straps on the pack, and fell into step beside Maren. His "would've been, should've been" missionary arrival fell into step beside him. Previous thoughts of the homecoming he had anticipated collided with his reality. The collateral damage flung shards of expected experiences against the foundation of his heart. It was all he could do to keep it from cracking. He wasn't in a white shirt and tie. There was no black missionary tag on his chest. Nothing set him apart as a missionary returning home. He simply looked like a nineteen-year-old guy traveling in blue jeans with a puffy face. *Blasted cancer.*

He neared the escalator and stepped on. He could see a few small groups gathering at the bottom of the moving staircase, each waiting for their arriving passenger. His eyes fell on a bright pink poster that said, "Welcome Home, Ricky!" and another poster right next to it that said, "We missed you!" He looked at the two young faces holding the posters and smiled. It was Lexi's younger sisters, Olivia and Aleah. Standing behind them was Emily and Kris. Ricky stepped off of the escalators and walked towards them. He hugged them, somewhat confused. As excited as he was to see them, he couldn't help but wonder where Lexi and his family were.

Without notice, a hoard of inflatable T-rexes came charging towards him from around the corner. Given their various sizes he could only guess it was Danja, his brothers, and Rick. After the initial mauling of air-filled tails and T-rex arms, he couldn't help but notice that there were two extra dinos in the herd. He worked his way through the smothering of dino hugs and finally had the chance to look at the clear vinyl opening in each costume. He discovered that the extra bodies occupying the dino suits belonged to Lexi and Cam. Ricky looked at Lexi, hair sticking up from the static cling generated from the blow-up dino suit, and just laughed at her.

"How am I even supposed to hug you in this thing?" Ricky asked.

Lexi laughed and did her best to wrap her tiny T-Rex arms around Ricky. It had only been a few short weeks since Ricky had expressed his true feelings to Lexi, yet his arms held her as if they were made to do so. He instinctively pulled her closer and Lexi's heart swelled. After his luggage was gathered, he slipped his hand into Lexi's and delighted at the fact that the motion felt just as comfortable as he remembered.

"I'm so excited for tonight, Mom," Lexi said as she looked through her closet to try to decide on an outfit to wear.

Emily sat on the bed and watched Lexi rifling through shirt after shirt. Lexi disregarded the traitorous clothes in frustration and looked at the articles with a sense of betrayal.

"I have nothing to wear," Lexi said with dramatic exacerbation.

"Why are you so nervous?" Emily asked with a smile. "You and Ricky have been on plenty of dates before."

"I'm not nervous," Lexi said, mildly defensive. Emily looked at her with raised eyebrows and motioned to the closet and the pile of discarded outfits that had not made the cut. Lexi let out a sigh and plopped her thin frame on the bed beside the perfidious apparel.

"I know that we've been on dates before, but this is our first date as boyfriend and girlfriend. Everything just feels different but in a good way. I'm not really nervous, just excited," Lexi said. Then she turned back to her closet and continued to go through her wardrobe hoping that something would magically appear that wasn't there before.

"Just breathe," Ricky reminded himself as he drove to Lexi's house. He had made this same drive numerous times, but now it wasn't just Lexi's house he was driving to, it was his girlfriend's house. Hopefully, it would one day soon be his fiancée's house. Ricky knew he would need to be patient, but he had never experienced anything like the impression he had that he and Lexi belonged together. It was all he could do to push the feeling aside while he was on his mission. But now, he was home, and it was all he could think about. From the moment that Ricky had told Lexi how he felt, he had the urge to share it with the world. He posted pictures of her on his social media and added her name to all of his bios. He needed everyone to know without a doubt that he was in love with Alexis Gould.

Ricky knocked on the brightly colored front door and he heard Aleah's excited voice on the other side. Lexi's youngest sister's eyes danced with excitement when she opened the door.

"Hi Ricky!" she said, "Lexi has been trying to decide all day what to wear for your date."

"Okay, Boo," Emily said as she guided Aleah away from the door and up the stairs. "Let's let Ricky come all the way in before you tease your sister anymore," Leah laughed and ran along, her golden curls bouncing freely behind her. Ricky smiled at the innocence of youth, but his smile caught when he saw Lexi. She had just walked down the hall and was now only ten feet from him. He blinked quickly, trying to focus on something other than this beautiful girl that had agreed to go on a date with him.

"Are you ready to go?" he managed to say.

Lexi smiled softly at him and nodded affirmatively. They said their goodbyes to Lexi's family and walked to the car hand in hand. Ricky hurried to open Lexi's car door. She smiled and thanked him as she got in. He got in the car and together they said a prayer. They drove to Arctic Circle to get ice cream. Rather than go inside the restaurant, they opted to stay in the car and talk. It was just like it had always been and Ricky knew he couldn't hold his feelings in any longer. Without warning his heart took over.

"Lex, I love you. I am going to marry you," he blurted out.

Lexi's heart panicked and shock took over. Ricky wanted to marry her. Lexi's heart was racing. She wasn't sure how long it had been since Ricky had spoken but she knew she needed to say something, and quickly.

"I could see that happening," was the only response she could muster up. *Really brain?* She'd watched all of those lame chick flicks and now when she needed something cute to say, the only thing that came was a casual shoulder shrug accompanied by, *I could see that happening?* Ugh. She couldn't help but notice Ricky's shoulders fall. Her heart mimicked the motion. It was plain that was not the response he was hoping for.

This was supposed to be the start of the conversation that led to how long he had loved her and where their future was headed. Instead, Ricky felt as if he had just released the game-winning jumper only to have it swatted at the buzzer.

Lexi's heart ached knowing that she had caused him pain. She opened her mouth but was unable to get the words out before Ricky went on.

"So, how's school going?" Ricky asked as he tried to play off his hurt and change the subject. Lexi responded generally as her heart continued to work through the previous conversation that hung between them. Why had she responded that way? She was so young and so uncertain of her future. Ricky's future seemed more fluid than it ever had. Should they really be talking about getting married on their first official date as boyfriend and girlfriend?

"How was the first official date?" Emily asked as Lexi carefully walked up the stairs.

"It was really great to be 'together, together' if that makes sense," Lexi said as she sat at the kitchen table and instinctively picked up the small vials of vitamins that were waiting to be injected into her nightly feeds. Suffering a small love crisis was no excuse to send her levels into a frenzy by ignoring her nightly nutrition.

"We had a great talk and he told me he is going to marry me," Lexi said.

"Hmmm," Emily replied as she fought an *I knew it* smile. "How do you feel about that?"

"I love him, Mom. I love him more than I ever thought possible. But . . ." She exhaled as she tried to keep her composure and find the right words to describe the turmoil she was facing.

"But what, honey?" Emily said gently.

"But, everything is so uncertain. He had so much going for him and had so many plans for his future. That may all change with his relapse, but maybe not. Maybe he will still be able to do everything he's always wanted to do. I hope so. But, it's not just his health I am worried about. I don't ever want to be the reason that he is not able to live the life that he has dreamt of. What if my cancer comes back? Not to mention, there's a good chance I won't be able to have children. I just don't want him to ever have to miss out on anything in life because he wants to marry me. He deserves more than that. He deserves more than I can give him." Lexi exhaled and softly added, "He deserves more than me."

A moment passed and she concluded, "He deserves the best. I just want him to have everything he deserves."

Emily's heart ached for her daughter. How could this beautiful, kindhearted soul ever think she was less than perfect for the man that had been in love with her for the past two years? But her worries were valid. She would face physical trials that others may not face in this life. There would be sadness and heartache, but that did not need to destroy the happiness and joy that was just beginning.

"Did you tell Ricky about any of this?" Emily asked softly.

"No," Lexi confessed. "I didn't know how to say it." Lexi looked down and saw the dainty gold chain that hung around her neck. She smiled softly and lightly touched it with her fingers. "He gave me this tonight," she said.

"It's beautiful," Emily remarked as she looked at the necklace.

"He gave me this and a beautiful jewelry box that he bought in New York. He put the necklace on me then kissed me and said that this was just the first piece of jewelry. I told him that I don't need jewelry to be happy. He hugged me and said he would spend his life making me happy."

"Hey Ricky," Lexi texted as she lay in bed that night. "I'm sorry that my words hurt you. This is just a lot right now and I am scared." Lexi felt more vulnerable than she had in a long time, that was until she read his response.

"I'm scared too, Lex. I don't know what my future holds. I can't promise you an exciting life, or even that I will be here for the rest of your life. I just know that as long as I am breathing, you are the person I want to be with. I want you forever. Only you. Do you know how much I really love you?"

Lexi reassured Ricky of her love for him, and he did the same for her. Before Ricky set his phone down for the night, he quickly typed out one more text.

"Hey Sister Gould, how long do you think I need to wait before I ask your daughter to marry me?" He smiled and hit send. Time was not a luxury that he and Lexi had. He needed to make the most of every minute.

Chapter 13

"It has always ever been you. To you, my heart belongs."
—Morgan Brady

Breathe. Ricky reminded himself. Just breathe. His left leg pulsed nervously as he sorted through the hurricane of words swirling around his brain. He exhaled and began to combine fragments of phrases to formulate sentences. Just then, Lexi walked into the room. His mind went blank as she smiled the smile that was meant only for him. The fury of words and nerves that had been brewing inside his head subsided with the presence of peace that she brought. She greeted him with a quick kiss and went to work choosing the dresses she would model for the photo shoot that day.

Several times over the last few years, Lexi had been asked to model for different photographers and organizations. Some shoots featured her fearless bald head glistening in the sun, others showcased her short pixie cut that was made complete by the soft chemo curls treatment had left her with. Whether the photographer posed her as a warrior highlighting her battle scars, or surrounded her delicate frame with soft evening gowns, Lexi seemed to deliver exactly what the camera was looking for. Ricky had often seen the proofs from the shoots that Lexi participated in. He never ceased to be amazed at the her physical beauty. Lexi's physical countenance came in second only to the strength of her spirit and the genuine love that she so freely emanated. However, this was Ricky's first time being featured alongside her.

Today's shoot was being put on by one of Lexi's favorite organizations. Celebrate Everyday was a nonprofit organization that had been founded by a young college student, Jocee, who was interested in helping others. This group had an inventory of hundreds of semi-formal and formal dresses that young people could borrow for free. The hope that each teenager would feel beautiful for their special occasions, regardless of their ability to purchase expensive dresses, was the motivating factor behind their establishment. Photo shoots were always a fun way to spend a few hours, but Lexi especially liked doing so for a good cause. Today she would be selecting her attire from the dresses that the organization offered. Her makeup would be done by an up-and-coming makeup artist, and two photographers would be certain that the entire afternoon would be captured from every angle. The photos would be placed on the organization's website. Ricky had been invited along to give social media the full effect of how the evening gowns would look in a "real date" setting.

For the last few months, the only thing that had been on Ricky's mind was how he would ask Lexi to be his wife. He recognized that he was only nineteen years old, but it felt like he had waited ten lifetimes to become Lexi's husband. He could not bring himself to wait any longer. Unbeknownst to Lexi, Ricky had formulated a plan. As soon as Lexi asked him to come along for the photo shoot, he had reached out to Jocee and asked her to be an active participant in the day's events. Jocee was so excited at the prospect of being part of a surprise proposal that she instantly agreed. She reached out to the photographers, the makeup artist, and the florist to make sure everyone was on board and ready to create the perfect event.

Ricky watched Lexi walk towards the racks of dresses and realized that if Lexi decided she was not ready to say yes to marrying him that day, he would ask her another day, and another, and a thousand times more until she was ready. He would do whatever it took to make sure that he got to spend the rest of eternity married to Alexis Gould.

Lexi gently ran her fingers over the soft fabric of the gowns. She smiled at the sequins, ruffles, and glittery material that her younger self would have been enamored with. Her gaze stopped at a mermaid style maroon dress. The satin fabric had thick straps and a fitted bodice that flared at the knee. The gown would fit Lexi's curves flawlessly and accentuate the weight she had worked so hard to put back on. Just a few dresses over she spotted a navy-blue gown. The simple style had thick straps that gathered and a beautiful, yet understated, rhinestone design on the front. Layers of sheer fabric gave the flowing dress a whimsical feel. Lexi glanced over her shoulder to see Ricky staring at her with a dreamy look in his eyes.

"Hi, My Love," Lexi said with a twinkle in her eye. "Why are you looking at me like that?" she teased him playfully, with one genuine eyebrow raised and a rueful smile at the edge of her mouth. "Is my hair sticking up again?" she asked as she ran her hair through her chin length locks.

"Your hair is perfect," he said. "You are perfect," he added, mesmerized by her.

"I'm so lucky to have you," she said, as she walked over and gave him a quick kiss. "Are you doing okay? You seem a little nervous."

Ricky's face went blank, and he nervously chuckled as he did his best to play it cool. His left leg kicked into overtime, and he swore that someone had turned the heater, and his heartbeat, up exponentially. Lexi was far too good at reading his emotions to not know that something was going on with him. He swallowed hard and found the best smile he had for the most perfect girl that had ever existed. She smiled back expectantly, still waiting for an answer.

"Is everything okay?" she asked again. "You look a little pale. I promise that photo shoots are nothing to be worried about," she added.

Ricky jumped to his feet a little too quickly and announced that he was doing just fine but suddenly felt the need to go on a walk. He quickly left the small room, stumbling over words and dress racks as he went, hoping Lexi hadn't figured out his plan already.

Lexi looked at Emily with a confused look on her face.

Emily shrugged her shoulders in hopes that the gesture would clear her of any further questioning. "Maybe he's just nervous because it's his first official photo shoot," Emily quickly offered. "He's not quite as comfortable with them as you are yet."

Lexi raised her existent eyebrow and wrinkled her forehead. She wasn't buying the weak excuse and Emily didn't blame her.

With dresses in tow, Lexi and Ricky loaded into his green Jetta and followed the procession of cars that included Jocee, the photographers, and the makeup artist. Emily and Maren, both aware of what was happening, had opted to drive together.

"Hey Babe, I love you," Ricky said as they drove to their destination.

"I love you, too, my Ricky Boy," Lex said as she gave his hand a squeeze.

"I really, really love you," Ricky said again, needing nothing more in this moment than for her to understand the tenderness that her presence exposed in him.

Lexi smiled and reassured him that the feelings were mutual.

"Lex, do you ever want to date anyone else?"

Lexi looked at Ricky questioningly. This topic had been addressed from every angle several times over the past two months. Regardless of the fact that they were both young, they had individually come to the conclusion that they wanted to spend the rest of their lives together.

"You already know the answer to that, My Love," Lexi said affectionately.

"Okay, but you are a hundred percent sure. Right?" he prodded.

"Of course I am sure," Lexi said simply. She was a girl who took her concerns to God; once she had an answer from Him, she continued forward unabated. She had prayed about Ricky, possibly more in depth than she had ever prayed for anything else. She knew without reserve that he was the person she would spend her life with.

"I pinky promise," Lexi said as she held up her slender little finger. "I love you and only you. Always."

Ricky held his pinky up in response and hooked it to Lexi's. "I love you and I love you more and I love you most. Only you. Forever." He held her gaze and added, "So, this means that you pinky promise to say yes when I ask you to marry me, right?" he said looking right at her.

Lexi laughed out loud. "Of course, I do!" She then lovingly added, "The light is green now, you need to stop looking at me and focus on the road, you maniac."

Ricky looked into her eyes, kissed her hand and proceeded to their destination with his focus mostly on the road.

The small cavalcade adjourned at "This is the Place Heritage Park" in Salt Lake City, Utah. They stepped out of their cars and were immediately struck with the bitterness of the cold. It was not a typical winter cold that one grows accustomed to in Utah. It was the type of cold that freezes a person down to their core and makes their bones ache. It was the kind of cold that is beautiful in landscapes and pictures, but meant only to be admired behind closed windows while cuddled in a warm blanket, sitting next to a fire. Knowing that they would be modeling prom attire for this photo shoot, Ricky had worn his suit. It wasn't helping. The bitterness permeated the linen fabric. Lexi, on the other hand, had on only the first of her two prom dresses.

Ricky's breath caught at the sight of Lexi in the flowing navy gown. The gathered sheer fabric bunched together to create thick straps that left her shoulders bare. The ink blue gown had an empire waist that accentuated Lexi's petite frame and then cascaded freely from her body. The gown was the ocean and Lexi's eyes the summer sky, each working in perfect harmony for Ricky to get lost in.

Lexi had a natural beauty that could not be denied, but the makeup artist had capitalized on that, highlighting each of her natural features. Her lashes were darker and fuller, her eyes a more intense blue. Her high cheekbones accented the soft angles of her face. The makeup artist had chosen to forgo the foundation in an effort to let Lexi's porcelain skin showcase her natural freckles. Lexi had opted to cover the PICC line that was still in her upper arm with some tan Coban gauze in hopes of having the tubes jutting out from her appendage be less obvious in the photos. Tubes or not, Ricky couldn't remember a time when she looked more perfect.

Ricky and Lexi took their lead from the photographer, walking from place to place stopping for pictures along the way. Lexi seemed to be at ease with the camera on her. Ricky watched as a quiet confidence befell her that manifested itself through the lens. Ricky, on the other hand, felt more vulnerable and exposed than he had in a long time. The medications he was taking had caused his jawline to disappear behind the soft fluff of the Prednisone moon face. He had treatment induced diabetes, his face looked worse than it had when he was thirteen, and he regularly vomited without warning. Unlike Lexi, his retching was far from silent.

Ricky was minutes away from asking the strongest, most beautiful girl he'd ever met to be his wife forever. His heartbeat quickened. He had cancer, not just in the past, but at this very moment. He was fighting for his life. That meant some ugly days were ahead. It wasn't just the certainty that he would lose his hair that bothered him. It was the knowledge that his body would once again become weak and compromised. He would be physically unable to be a good boyfriend most days, let alone a good husband. How would he financially provide and care for Lexi when he couldn't even take care of himself? Just as she was getting better and had the opportunity to get on with her life, he had come home early from his mission. He was now going to ask her to marry him and ask her to jump headfirst into what felt like a downward spiral.

"This is your last chance, Lex," Ricky said, trying to mask his nerves with a mockingly serious tone, followed by a short laugh.

"Last chance for what?" Lexi said as she looked at him with her piercing blue eyes. They sparkled as if to play with his heart, but he noticed that they held a deeper worry, as if she knew he was more concerned with something than he was letting on.

"This is your last chance to back out and move on with your life before you are stuck with me forever," he said with a quick laugh.

"I'm not going anywhere," Lexi replied easily. She swore she heard him exhale and, grinning deeply, she added, "We pinky promised."

His easy smile reached his eyes and his hand tightened around hers as he spun her around to the clicking of cameras. She laughed, despite the cold, as he placed his hand behind her back and dipped her. She could hear the clicking of the cameras but could see only Ricky's inky cyan eyes locked on hers. He held her gaze and she saw the depth of his love for her reflected in his eyes. The clicking of the cameras faded. He smiled softly at her, and she looked up at him. He took the opportunity to steal a kiss that made the world disappear.

"That is pure gold!" the photographer said as she moved in closer and began circling to the other side of the couple.

"You two are perfect!" the second photographer echoed.

The comments brought Ricky and Lexi back to the realization that they were not the only people in the gazebo. Ricky spun Lexi around for a few more photos and held her tight for some close ups.

"I think we have everything we need from this dress," Jocee said. "Lex, let's try to unthaw you a bit and then get some shots in the second one." Ricky reluctantly let his hand slide from the small of

Lexi's back. He quickly shed his suit coat and placed it around Lexi's shoulders. His hand habitually found a home in hers and they walked back to the cars together.

The modeling of the first dress was complete and Lexi was changing into the dress she would be wearing when Ricky would ask her to be his wife. He sat in his car, willing the sensation to return to his limbs. Maren turned the radio up and they found their rhythm with a familiar Eminem song. Ricky recalled the times that the same song had been used to hype him up before a game or to lift his spirits during treatment, but this—this was something different. This was more than a game or a round of chemo. This was the rest of his eternity, and Lexi's if she said yes.

Anxiety and worry clouded his brain. He forced them aside and filled his thoughts with Lexi. The only thing he knew for certain was that she was meant for him and he for her. They belonged together like two halves of a whole, two sides of a coin, two souls drawn together despite all odds. They were meant to be. The thought brought Ricky peace and his heartbeat returned to normal, until Lexi stepped into sight wearing a maroon mermaid-style gown that hugged the curves of her frame perfectly. The form-fitting dress broke free from its restraints and flared out just above Lexi's knees.

The sun was evident in the sky but had no effect on the temperature. Ricky's teeth chattered and he could only imagine how frigid Lexi must be feeling. She huddled close to him as he placed his suit coat over her shoulders once again. He put his arm around her and pulled her close to him. They walked to the nearest gazebo for the next set of photos.

The ring in Ricky's pants pocket seemed to weigh a metric ton and he wondered briefly if the small box was visible to anyone else. It appeared to have a homing beacon on it that synced with his heartbeat. The small entourage arrived at the gazebo and the photographer positioned them. Lexi gave Ricky his jacket back with a quick kiss. Ricky smiled and stole another kiss as the cameras began their clicking. Ricky held Lexi close and then spun her around amidst her laughter.

"That's great!" encouraged the photographer. "Keep doin' what you are doing!"

Lexi laughed as Ricky tickled her playfully.

"Let's get a few close ups with this dress. Lex, you look absolutely stunning," the photographer said.

Ricky put his arms around Lexi's waist as they both faced the camera. He gently kissed her cheek and she turned to smile at him softly. Once again, everything faded away. The clicking of the cameras was silenced by Ricky's heartbeat. The frigid air, by the warmth of Lexi's body next to his.

"Guys, hey guys?" They were brought back to the moment by Jocee. Ricky heard a few giggles and a couple comments about young love, but he paid no mind to any of it.

"Ricky, I want you to stand in the back of the gazebo and just look at Lex."

"Not a problem," Ricky said far too quickly. More laughter followed so he added, "Looking at her is one of my favorite things to do."

Ricky gave Lex a quick hug and kissed her on the top of her chestnut hair. The photographer positioned Ricky and quietly gave him a nod, letting him know that everything was in position for him to make his move. He backed up and the cameras began to click.

"Look right at me," the photographer said. "Ricky, you just look at Lexi."

"You don't have to tell me twice," Ricky responded with a wiggle of his brows. "Have you seen her?" The group laughed collectively as the cameras continued their clicking.

"Look down and to the left, Lex. Yes, that is perfect."

"Okay, now look this way."

"Lex, can you run your fingers through your hair."

The comments continued as Ricky gently pulled the ring from his pocket and gingerly opened the box. He let his knee drop to the frozen wood of the gazebo.

"Okay Lex, we are going to have you turn around very slowly and look at Ricky," said the photographer.

Lexi followed the instructions like a pro. Carefully she turned her shoulders and hips towards Ricky and then allowed her head to follow suit. Her gaze found Ricky's and her jaw went slack. Both of her hands instinctively covered her gaping mouth as she let out a little laugh.

"Wait," she said while shaking her head slightly. "Wait, is this real life?" She looked around to see the smiles of faces amid the clicking of cameras. "Is this really real?" she repeated.

"Yeah, this is real," said Ricky, impatiently waiting for an answer to a question that he realized he never actually asked.

"Are you serious?" Lexi asked incredulously. She moved her hands from her mouth just long enough to speak. "Is this just part of the photo shoot?"

"This is real, Lex," Ricky repeated. "Will you marry me?" Lexi's hands covered her mouth, once again, as Ricky nervously added, "You pinky promised."

Lexi laughed right out loud. "Yes!" she said through a beaming smile. "Of course I will marry you!"

Ricky unleashed the breath of air he had held captive. He got to his feet and carefully placed a simple diamond band on Lexi's slender left ring finger. He kissed Lexi excitedly and then held her close, basking in the knowledge he would never have to let her go. Ricky felt as if his jubilation would boil over and without warning he picked Lexi up and spun her around. They were surrounded by the symphony of her laughter and the soft hum of clicking cameras.

Chapter 14

"Sometimes being a brother is even better than being a superhero" —Marc Brown

Despite the excitement that an engagement brought, the reality of what Ricky needed to overcome was daunting. He often felt like he was lucky when it came to his first diagnosis, not that it was easy, but the more he saw what other people with cancer went through, the more he was grateful for the aspects of treatment he was able to avoid. However, that would not be the case this time around.

In addition to chemo, Ricky's treatment plan would also consist of full-body radiation and a bone marrow transplant. Radiation looked different for him than it did for Lexi. Rather than laying in a full body mold, Ricky stood. An odd-looking contraption known as an "iron lung" was placed over his chest area in hopes of minimizing the damaging effects of radiation. Although Lexi had often referred to radiation as a break in her treatment, it had the opposite impact on Ricky. The treatment caused nausea, pain, and general discomfort that he was not fully prepared for. However, as was the case with the majority of cancer treatments, the short-term effects paled in comparison to the long-term effects that awaited the patient. These effects included but were not limited to heart disease and irregularity, issues with the endocrine system, kidney, and lungs, as well as, osteoporosis, infertility, and an increased risk of relapse or secondary cancer brought on by the radiation.

Lexi opened the door to the Stafford home and climbed the three stairs into the open floor plan. She was greeted with a hug by the younger boys, and quickly found Ricky lying on the couch in the family's living room. He was in the fetal position and groaning, almost imperceptibly. Without hesitation, Lexi went to his side. She wrapped her arms lovingly around him and spoke softly. Ricky felt his muscles begin to relax at her touch and his hurt dissipate in her presence. Lexi gently wiped the tears of pain that had managed to escape unnoticed.

"Babe, I don't know if I can do this," he whispered to her, trying to hold back any subsequent tears. "I am in so much pain. I don't know if my body can do this."

"You can do this, My Love," Lexi reassured him. "I will be right here. You don't have to do any of it alone. I know you're hurting, and I know it's hard. But I know that you can do this. We can do this. I've got you." Lexi stayed until Ricky had drifted into a comfortable sleep and then repeated the process throughout radiation.

After radiation, Ricky would need a bone marrow transplant or BMT. The concept of a BMT was very similar to that of a stem cell transplant. He would receive a week of fatal chemo and then he'd be given cells from a donor that mostly closely matched his bone marrow. He'd seen just a handful of the horrors that accompanied transplant when Lexi went through hers. The thought of what his own might hold was debilitating.

Sherman Abrahm Stafford, or "Abe" as he had always been called, sighed heavily as he looked at his young hands. The long fingers had grown since the first time he heard that his brother could die. He wrung them together nervously as he looked around his sterile surroundings. In the distance, he heard the beeping of a monitor through the thin blue walls. Abe allowed the memories of Ricky's first cancer diagnosis to flood his mind. Perhaps the rush of uncharted emotions would be enough to drown the worry that was building inside of him. Abe had only been seven years old when Ricky was first diagnosed with cancer. It was a lifetime ago, but somehow felt like just yesterday when the oldest of the Stafford village came home from the doctor's office with a dumbfounded look on his face.

It had been a typical weekday in the Stafford home. Life was abuzz with young boys running in and out, while Danja, the second oldest and only sister, searched for her other shoe in hopes of finding it quickly enough to be on time to basketball practice. Tinka, the family dog, roamed aimlessly around the open floor plan of the house while Hyrum and Till, only five and three years old respectively, looked for their next grand adventure. Abe had just gotten back from school and was looking for something to eat that would produce maximum calories with minimum effort. He was always hungry these days, maybe he was getting ready to go on another growth spurt. Heaven knows the calories never went to his angular frame.

The front door opened and Maren walked in, seeming not to process the familiarity of the comfortable chaos that accompanied the Stafford home. Ricky followed in a daze behind her. He looked around the house as if he was trying to commit every object to memory, animate and inanimate alike. His jaw quivered as he watched his younger brothers wrestle shirtless on the front room floor. He tightened his features and headed solemnly up to his room.

Abe heard a knock that was followed by the opening of the front door. Nana, Maren's mom, walked into the kitchen first, her bright smile was ever present on her face, but it did not seem to reach her eyes today. Grandpa, Maren's dad, followed close behind, his quick-witted humor replaced with a melancholy feeling that matched that of Ricky and Maren. Abe did not understand the reason behind the storm cloud of emotion that hung heavy over his home, at least not until he heard the word *cancer*. The word was foreign to him. Obviously he knew what cancer was, but why would anyone in his family be talking about it? The Stafford family was known for their physical traits, a characteristic that had been carried over from generations before.

Cancer was a physical abnormality, a weakness, something that didn't happen to families like theirs. Cancer was something that people got when they were old, or if they had a lot of other health problems. His family wasn't like other families he thought. They had a legacy of physical health and athleticism that went back generations. They focused on physical traits and prided themselves on competition. They didn't get hurt or sick the way that other families did. But, the look on Ricky's face said something different. Abe silently observed the scene unfolding before him.

Over the next hour, a few aunts and uncles dropped in, but the rivalry that usually accompanied family events were nowhere to be found. The family gathered in the living room, the adults with tear stains streaking down their cheeks like water cutting into rock. The kids were vying for a spot on the couch but ultimately found their respite on the hardwood floor. A chair had been placed in the middle of the living room and Ricky slowly made his way to it. Ricky's eyes were swollen from tears he must've cried, although Abe never saw them. His gaze seemed far away, as if he were hoping to be anywhere but where he was. He caught Abe's glance and gave him a small smile that seemed to take far too much effort. Abe stared at his older brother and simply returned the smile.

Ricky closed his eyes as hands were placed upon his fifteen-year-old head. Ricky felt the weight of the strong hands that faltered in comparison to the weight of his situation. Abe looked around confusedly. Was Ricky really the one that was sick? It wasn't possible. Ricky was strong and healthy. He played basketball. He couldn't even drive yet and he was already 6'2". Abe knew that Ricky had been feeling weak. He remembered just a few days before how the boys were all out shoveling snow. Ricky had been too weak to lift his shovel. After a few jokes from his brothers and some frustration from his parents about his inability to be strong, Ricky ended up going inside to rest. Abe had thought he just didn't want to help shovel the walks anymore. Abe looked at Ricky now. Ricky looked tired. He didn't look that sick. Definitely not sick enough to have cancer. Abe shook his head at the naive ignorance of his seven-year-old self. Not every kid that had cancer looked like they had cancer.

A blessing was given to Ricky. Young Abe thought he saw a drop of water escape one of Ricky's eyes but couldn't be sure. The longer this scene played out, the more unnatural it all felt. Abe watched Ricky stand slowly and hug each of his uncles, his grandpa, and finally Rick. Ricky then solemnly turned and walked up the stairs. A few minutes later, Ricky returned with a small duffle bag. He hugged each of his siblings and turned towards the door. Rick followed suit. The sound of the door echoed in the oddly quiet house, as if the bones of the home itself understood the heaviness of the moment.

It didn't take long for the Stafford family to adjust to Ricky's diagnosis. The months following that fateful day consisted of Ricky being in and out of the hospital. Some days he was at home and a part of life, some days he was not. Regardless, life in the Stafford home continued on, wrestling matches were won and lost, basketball games were played, and hurty games were participated in. Danja had stepped up as honorary caregiver, a calling that seemed natural to her motherly nature.

One day, Rick called the family into the kitchen. Ricky sat looking a bit round faced, and weird, if Abe was being honest. Eyebrows did more for Ricky's appearance than Abe had realized. Abe really hoped he never lost all of his hair and eyebrows. On the other hand, Ricky had been getting a lot of attention and extra treats from people. Abe considered both sides of the coin. He still wasn't sure it was worth being bald. The family gathered at the island in their kitchen area. The bare-chested boys grappled at a spot at one of the stools but ultimately found themselves standing.

"The doctors told us today that Ricky might need a bone marrow transplant," Rick said. The kids looked at one another to see if any of them had actually understood why this was something that they needed to be aware of.

"Okay," Danja said, with hesitation. "So what does that mean?" Danja, being the closest to Ricky in age, had a natural inclination to help in any way that she could. Her heart found solace in caring for her younger brothers, but she often wished she could do more to personally help Ricky. She never let her worries escape her mouth for fear of the added stress it would bring to her family, but the thought of him dying from cancer kept her awake at night.

"Well, he will need someone to donate their bone marrow to him." Rick stopped and gauged the looks on the faces of his young family. Ricky, being the oldest, was only fifteen. Cyrus, the youngest, was only one. These were not conversations that young children should ever have to be involved in. When none of them responded, he continued on.

"We would like each of you to get your blood drawn so that we can see who would be the best match." One by one the young siblings nodded their heads in agreement. The kids looked at each other nervously. Without another word, Rick responded with finality. "Okay," He said decisively and the conversation turned to upcoming games and events. No one wanted to talk about cancer. It wasn't fun.

Within the next few weeks, the Stafford crew loaded up their white fifteen passenger van and headed up to Primary Children's hospital. Abe's seven-year-old self sat on the crinkly plastic next to Hyrum and Till. The twins, Radi and Eli, kept fighting over a chair while Danja sat in the other one. Being the only girl had its perks. Rick looked at the boys with one brow raised in warning. Radi gave Eli a passing jab and settled on the floor.

A nurse entered the room with a tray full of test tubes. One by one, each sibling was subjected to the unpleasant sting of a needle entering their skin. Even Cyrus, the baby, would not be spared the poke. Not wanting to show weakness, the boys refused to react to the unfamiliar pinch. The sight of the blood, however, was another story. They all began to be extremely interested in what shade of blue the opposite wall was.

Abe was the oldest, closest match. He didn't fully understand what that meant, but, luckily he never had to. His willingness to be Ricky's donor was enough. Ricky got better and Abe wouldn't have to be poked with any more needles. It was a win-win situation. Ricky went on his mission and left his cancer behind. Then, without warning, the cancer came back. Abe was at a loss. Staffords don't get cancer, let alone twice. After getting the news that Ricky had relapsed, Rick knew that his son would not be spared transplant twice in one lifetime. Rick approached Abe one day after school.

"How do you feel about having the opportunity to save your brother's life?" Rick asked his son. Abe somberly nodded his head affirmatively, and without further discussion, the conversation switched to basketball.

Abe blinked hard and returned to the present. He was now in the seventh grade. He was a gangly 5'8" with limitless potential for physical growth. His curly hair and soft brown eyes worked well together. Ricky might be Rick Stafford's namesake, but Abe was the physical carbon copy of his father. His young mind had spent the previous month anxiously researching and reading everything the internet had to offer regarding bone marrow transplants and the effects of being a bone marrow donor.

According to Google, a bone marrow transplant was "done by transferring stem cells from one person to another. Stem cells could either be collected from the circulating cells in the blood (the peripheral system) or from the bone marrow. Peripheral blood stem cells (PBSCs) are collected by apheresis." Seemed pretty cut and dry to Abe's almost thirteen-year-old brain. They were going to take the healthy stuff from him and give it to Ricky. *Okay*, he thought. *But, how exactly are they going to do that?* "Bone marrow donation is a surgical procedure that takes place in a hospital operating room. Doctors use needles to withdraw liquid marrow (where the body's blood-forming cells are made) from both sides of the back of your pelvic bone. You will be given anesthesia and feel no pain during the donation." *Ugh. Needles.* Abe thought as he shivered involuntarily. At least they were going to give him anesthetic so he wouldn't be awake for any of it.

Abe's mind continued with the questions. *How long will it take before I start to feel all the way better? I have a life to live, too.* "Marrow and PBSC donors should expect to return to work, school, and most other activities within 1 to 7 days. Your marrow will return to normal levels within a few weeks." *Okay, good,* Abe thought. He could handle a week of taking things easy. If he were lucky, he might even get out of a few chores.

All in all, the whole thing didn't sound too bad. Abe continued reading just to be certain he wasn't missing anything. "The risks of this type of stem cell donation are minimal. Before the donation, you'll get injections of a medicine that increases the number of stem cells in your blood. This medicine can cause side effects, such as bone pain, muscle aches, headache, fatigue, nausea and vomiting." Okay, so maybe it wouldn't be a complete break from everything, but a little pain and throwing up actually sounded a bit more appealing than cleaning a bathroom in a house with seven boys. He really hoped this gave him a pass from chores for at least a week. Over the coming weeks, Abe endured more doctor appointments than he had gone to over the course of his entire life. Each appointment promised more blood draws and some type of tests he couldn't pronounce.

It was 3 a.m. on the day of the donation. Abe groggily rolled out of bed. He pulled a shirt over his head and slipped on his shoes. He tried to open the fridge before Maren stopped his intentions with the reminder that he wasn't allowed to eat until after the procedure. He grumbled something about not being able to save Ricky's life if he starved to death first. His murmuring yielded nothing but stern looks from his mom. He lowered the tone of his grumbling and headed to the car.

Once they arrived at the hospital, Abe and Maren were taken to a room where they were given instructions and information on what their day, and the subsequent days, would look like for Abe. A nurse entered the sterile blue walls.

"I'm going to start your IV," she said cheerfully, as if she derived some sense of purpose by poking people with sharp objects. If this was her passion in life, she should reconsider her goals. Abe's stomach grumbled. The doctor reminded him, again, that he couldn't eat before the procedure. His stomach growled again in protest. He couldn't remember the last time he was this hungry. The too-cheery nurse chuckled at Abe's starvation and without warning she jabbed the needle into his helpless arm.

"Oops, it looks like I missed. I'm sorry about that," the nurse said. She didn't look sorry. She almost looked as if she were enjoying this. She rooted the needle around in his arm like a blind squirrel hunting for a nut on a dark winter night.

"Hmmm," she said, a bit perplexed. Abe wasn't sure why she should be perplexed when he was the one being used as a human pincushion. At last, she pulled the needle up and asked Abe to hold a cotton ball on the top of his hand to keep any blood that dripped from making a mess. A few minutes later, Nurse Cheery came back with reinforcements. A single reinforcement, to be exact.

"This is the Vein Sniper," the cheery nurse said, gesturing to the newcomer. Abe wasn't sure if he should be impressed or scared. This woman had a kind smile, but her eyes were focused in a way that Abe wondered if veins were the only thing she sniped. She took Abe's other hand in hers with a bit more force than Nurse Cheery had used. He looked away as The Sniper plunged the needle into his hand. Without warning, she began moving the needle around under his skin. He heard some small talk between the two nurses and realized that his veins proved impervious to the experienced antics of the infamous Vein Sniper. With each poke, each miss, Abe could feel his heartbeat escalate. His nerves compounded and a sickly feeling rose in his stomach. He told his thirteen-year-old self that it was nothing more than the consequence of not eating, but he knew better. He was worried. The longer his body refused the IV, the more time he had to dwell on the upcoming procedure and the twelve inch hollow needle that accompanied it.

"We will just have to call in the Pros," The Sniper said. The Pro Team came in with a small flashlight that they held to Abe's hand. The small light was pressed against his skin and he could see the veins in his hand. Before he could worry what would happen if they were unsuccessful, Abe felt a pinch and then felt the Pros stabilizing his newly placed IV with gauze and bandages. It was not long after that Nurse Cheery came in to take Abe to the procedure room. Abe sauntered down the hall in his hospital issue gown, grateful that the ties in the back seemed to be secure. He climbed onto the cold table and a new nurse offered him a warm blanket.

"Can you count down from ten for me?" the new nurse asked. Abe was starting to miss Nurse Cheery. People in this room were far more formal. Abe began as instructed, "10, 9, 8, 7, 6 . . ."

Abe awoke to the ache in his lower back. He heard himself groan, or at least someone who sounded like him. His head was foggy and he couldn't be sure of anything at that moment. He could see Maren's phone and heard her laughing. He must've been saying or doing something that was funny. He was sure he would hear about it later. For now, he knew only two things: his lower back was killing him, and his stomach felt so sick that he may never want to eat again.

"The anesthetic can make you feel sick, Abe," he heard Lexi say.

Up until this time he had thought she was still on the fourth floor with Ricky. She must've come down to see how he was doing. Without warning, Abe wretched. Luckily, Lexi had anticipated the reaction and was already there holding a garbage can. She rubbed his back and assured him that this feeling wouldn't last forever. Then she added, "Thank you for saving Ricky's life, Bird."

Today was the day. Abe was already downstairs in the procedure room. Soon, a nurse would enter Ricky's room with his brother's bone marrow that would save Ricky's life. The last week of chemo had been brutal. Ricky had vomited more than he ever thought possible. Lexi found a way to balance school, drill, work, and making sure she was at the hospital every day with Ricky. While most high school seniors were picking out prom dresses and planning dates, Lexi was doing homework next to a hospital bed and wondering how her mom had survived on hospital cafeteria food for two straight years. Lexi's own experience with cancer had taught her enough tips and tricks over the past few years, that she seemed to know what he needed before he needed it. She held his hand, made sure that he always had ice chips, and spent countless hours watching basketball games with him just to pass the time.

Lexi was now a senior in high school. She would graduate in just a few months. Her hair was down to her shoulders now and she was healthier than she had been in years. She had been able to dance with her drill team at a few school events and was working tirelessly to graduate with her class. Her job was going well and she had begun applying to colleges. She planned to complete her generals and then continue on to become a pediatric oncology nurse. Life was unfolding beautifully for her.

Ricky looked at her through groggy eyes. She could be anywhere in the world right now; she could be with anyone. Yet, somehow she chose him. She felt his eyes and looked over at him lovingly.

"Hi Babe, how are you doing?" Lexi's soft voice brought comfort to Ricky's battered body.

"I'm not feeling too good. Honestly, I'm hurting pretty bad and these mouth sores feel like they are just getting worse," he said, with effort. How had Lex gone through this twice? He felt as if there was a good chance he might not make it through once.

"They probably are going to keep getting worse for another week or so. Then, Abe's cells will engraft and you'll start feeling a bit better." They both knew that there was a chance Ricky's body wouldn't accept Abe's cells. They both knew that if that happened it meant a host of other problems in the very near future. They both knew nothing was guaranteed in life, especially in the cancer world. They both knew that whatever life held, they would face it together. Lexi changed the ice in the packs that rested on his face. She got him new heat packs and fresh ice chips to suck on. She arranged his pillows and adjusted his blankets to make sure he was comfortable. She then pulled a chair next to his bed and took his outstretched hand in hers.

"Abe is out of the procedure and is doing okay. He has some pain and nausea but they said everything went well. He and your parents are going to come up to see you before heading home." Ricky made a weak attempt at squeezing her hand to thank her. She gently rubbed her thumb against the back of his hand. "Also, I got you some root beer barrels to suck on when they do the transplant. It helps take the smell of creamed corn out of the air a bit," Lexi said as she held up a bag of the brown candies. Ricky smiled and did his best to thank her again. She really did think of everything.

It had been just a few weeks since Abe had donated his bone marrow to save Ricky's life, a fact that he felt he could use against Ricky for at least the next decade. He had been light-headed off and on and experienced a bit more pain than he had expected, but overall he felt as if his recovery was going well.

It was now March, and was the end of track season. Track played a close second to basketball on Abe's favorite sports list. He regularly competed in the high jump, the eight hundred meter sprint, and the mile. He had yet to finish a full practice since donation day, but he was not about to miss this week's meet. Alpine Days was a two-day event that was well recognized as one of the largest multi-school meets in Utah. Athletes from all over the state would be there and Abe was right on track to beat them all. Each Stafford in his family had to find a way to make a name for themselves in an athletic event. Acceptable sports included track, basketball, and wrestling. Luckily for Abe, he had excelled in track all year. This was his time to shine.

Abe's body still felt foggy. Everyday activities took too much energy. Tying his shoes, climbing the stairs, even walking around school caused him fatigue. His bones ached as if he were an old man. The BMT was three weeks ago, his healthy body should have recovered by now. Maybe it was all in his head. Maybe he just needed to tell himself to buck up and force his body to do what he knew it was capable of. Abe was determined to not only finish today, but to win. This was something he had practiced all year for. In a family full of athletes, Abe would take his place with this victory. He could already see the pride on his parents' faces.

Abe knelt and placed his right foot in the block, the left foot followed suit. He heard the gun signaling that the race had begun. His mind had reacted, but the fact that he was already behind in the race was a strong indication that he had not moved as fast as he thought he had. Abe pushed harder. His muscles groaned in protest and he responded with a mental command to move faster. Despite his efforts, he watched helplessly as his competitors got farther and farther away. They were running on air. He was stuck in quicksand. Abe began to see spots. His head swirled and he felt as if he might black out. He willed his legs forward and finally crossed the finish line. In fifteenth place.

Abe went home defeated and frustration sunk in. Why was this happening? Why did Ricky have to get sick and need a transplant during the most important time of his seventh-grade life? In time, his anger gave way to determination. Tomorrow was a new day, and he would come home a champion. He had to. He'd practiced. He'd prayed. He'd done what was right and saved his brother's life. Surely, he would be blessed for all of his efforts.

Abe walked over to warm up for his final event—the high jump. He took a breath and managed to clear a few small jumps, but he felt the struggle in his muscles. The competition began. Abe pushed himself—harder than he should have had to. He barely cleared the pole. With each round, his body grew more and more exhausted. It had come down to just Abe and one other competitor. Abe began his approach. The bar was set at five-foot-six. This was a no-brainer. He had cleared this height countless times before. He would clear it now. His mind told his body to jump, but his feet felt as if he was wearing ankle weights. He felt the scrape of the bar on his back as he curved over it and fell dejectedly onto the mat, the bar following suit. He had scratched his jump.

Abe watched anxiously as his opponent began his approach. He stared at the young man with a prayer in his heart. He knew it wasn't right to pray for others to fail. But he wanted so badly to succeed. Abe watched the young man jump and then saw the bar wiggle from contact with the pole. It fell to the ground. The judges looked at their sheets. Moments later it was announced that Abe held the tiebreaker between the two young athletes. He had won, but not how he wanted to. He was supposed to go down in a blaze of glory—setting a new personal best (if not a new state record). Instead, he had failed just one less time than someone else. This victory was tainted. He didn't perform how he wanted. He couldn't push himself like he wanted. He didn't win the way he had wanted.

Abe smiled as expected when they gave him his medal. But it felt too heavy. The leaden circle hung densely around his neck as frustration and doubt pulled at his heart. He'd practiced. He'd prayed. The same questions that hummed through his mind the night before, now shouted at his psyche. He'd done what was right and saved his brother's life. Why was this happening? Why did Ricky have to get sick and need a transplant during the most important time of his seventh-grade life?

In the coming days, Abe's vision of what victory looked like changed. He spent time hanging out with Ricky. He saw the way Ricky was having an even harder time recovering from the transplant than he was. Ricky was now completely bald, again, and had lost more weight. He vomited regularly and struggled going up the stairs. Yet, somehow, he was the brother that Abe most identified with. The two of them laughed, watched basketball, and talked about life. Abe may have been angry about how his track season ended, but his heart held nothing but gratitude for Ricky still being alive. Sure, Abe hadn't had his moment in the sun like he had planned, but he still had his big brother. His body would recover from this momentary setback, and probably become even stronger than it was before. But, even if it didn't, he knew in his heart that he had made the right choice.

Chapter 15

"You Will Forever Be My Always"

"I'm here," Ricky heard Lexi say. Out of reflex he tried to turn ever so slightly. The need he had to hold Lexi every time she was near him was too strong to ignore. But, Jen, ever the professional, caught him just in time.

"Okay Ricky, Lex is here now but don't turn around just yet," Jen said. The seasoned photographer had a way of putting people at ease with her calming spirit, but Ricky felt as if the anticipation of a thousand Christmas times would dwindle in comparison to the sheer excitement coursing through his veins right now.

"How about now?" Ricky asked as his fists clenched and unclenched with excitement. His toes wiggled in his maroon Converse shoes as he did his best to calm his overactive nerves.

"Not quite yet," Jen said. "I'm sorry, we are just finishing setting up the camera so that we can get the picture. I promise you can see Lexi in just a minute. Trust me, she is worth the wait."

Ricky's smile widened at the thought of Lexi. He fidgeted with his tie trying to keep his hands busy while he waited. He closed his eyes and exhaled. One week, only one more week and his forever would begin with the most amazing woman he knew.

Hikers passed on the trail and a slight breeze blew. It really was the perfect day in the mountains. The eagerness was palpable as Lexi noticed Ricky's hand clench and unclench in excitement. Jen was fluttering around making sure that the angles would be perfect. Emily had fixed and refixed Lexi's hair for the hundredth time only to decide to let the wind take it where it may. After what seemed like an eternity, Jen finally spoke some instructions.

"Okay, you two. I'm going to have Lexi back up about six feet and then slowly walk towards you. Then she will tap you, Ricky, then you can turn around."

It had been only a few short months since Ricky had proposed to Lexi. Their engagement was filled with health and hospital stays, magic and medications, escapades and education, treatment and timeless memories. Lexi had graduated high school and had completed her training to become a CNA. She currently worked in a care facility and was an obvious favorite of all of her patients. Ricky had finished treatment and his hair was coming back nicely. Their engagement did not follow the typical route of young love, but their lives had failed to follow that pattern as well.

The fresh mountain air entered his radiation-damaged lungs, and Ricky felt as if he had swallowed an entire jar of butterflies. This was it. The first time he would see Lexi in her dress—the dress she would be wearing as his bride. Ricky clenched his fists and let them go rapidly as the anticipation continued to build. His face felt as if it would split right in two if he smiled any wider. Just when he thought he couldn't take one more second, he felt the slightest tap on his shoulder. He slowly turned and stared openly at Lexi. Her white dress was simple. She did not need adornments. It contoured precisely to the shape of her strong body and slightly flared at the bottom accentuating that the weight she had put on had settled in the exact spots it should have. She raised one eyebrow flirtingly and Ricky's heart dropped. Without warning, his exhilaration turned to something so much more. He was no longer just a young man very excited to be marrying a beautiful girl. He was a man who had found the woman of his dreams, a woman that had seen him at his worst and loved him through all of it, a woman who he could share all of his emotions with; his best friend and eternal companion In just one week she would be his wife for all of eternity. The feeling hit him so hard that he could do nothing more than wrap Lexi in his arms and sob without restraint, grateful for the opportunity he had to spend the rest of forever with her.

Lexi held Ricky tight as the emotions coursed through him. He pulled back slightly to look into her intense azure eyes. She gently wiped his tears and softly kissed him. "I love you so much, Lex," Ricky softly whispered.

"I love you more," she gently responded.

"I love you more and I love you most," he countered. "Only you. Always will." He smiled softly as she brought her soft hand to his face and placed it on his cheek. He bent forward ever so slightly, brought her lips closer to his, and before kissing her added, "Forever."

It took all of Ricky's physical determination to not take Lexi straight from the first look to the courthouse to marry her right then. He could hardly stand the thought of spending one more minute without her physically with him. The following Saturday came, and Ricky and Lexi were married for time and all eternity in the Mount Timpanogos Temple of The Church of Jesus Christ of Latter-day Saints. They exited the double doors of the temple with both of their hands in the air, their excitement at being together too big to be physically contained. Ricky pulled Lexi in close and put his hand tightly around her small waist. He dipped her backwards and kissed his wife to the cheers of their families and closest friends.

Their reception was an event filled with twinkling lights strewn between large trees and around multiple gazebos. Pictures of their life journey together over the past three years were hung throughout the outdoor venue. The outdoor s'mores bar was a big hit with guests of all ages. The receiving line extended well into the parking lot, but after two hours the line was disbanded and the reception more closely resembled a tremendous gathering. Lexi's small cancer friends were in attendance, as were several mascots from a foundation that she regularly promoted. Nurses and doctors were as much of the celebration as family and friends. Together, the two of them cut their wedding cake. Ricky thought for a moment that he might gingerly feed the cake to his new bride, but he should have known better than that. Lexi smiled at him with challenge in her eyes. Before he knew it, Ricky had frosting all over his face. He grabbed Lexi amid her giggles. She squealed as he kissed her repeatedly, frosting face and all. The day was spent with copious amounts of unbridled laughter, uninhibited dancing, and unending love.

As the night drew to a close, Lexi retreated to the dressing room to change into her going away outfit. The dusty-blue dress fit her healthy frame perfectly and she said a silent prayer for the way that her body had bounced back from everything it had endured. Ricky took her hand and kissed it, then kissed her lips once again. Their family and friends had lined the path to their car and sparklers had been lit. Ricky and Lexi ran hand in hand through the path, laughing as they did. Their adventure had just begun.

"Do you think we should talk about it?" Ricky asked softly.

"I don't know what to say," Lexi replied quietly with her head sagging low. Her chin nearly rested on her chest as she studied the backs of her hands. The unspoken subject hung knowingly between them like a thick cloud of smoke making it difficult to see, to breathe, to find a way out.

Lexi couldn't bring her eyes to meet Ricky's gaze. She could feel his heart breaking and it caused her physical pain. This was her sickness, her weakness, and it was breaking him. She kept her head low and worked to keep her breathing even.

"Lex, look at me. Please, look at me," he said.

Slowly, her glistening blue eyes lifted and met his tear-filled ones.

"Talk to me, Lex. What are you thinking?"

They sat facing one another on the floor in their basement apartment. The small room was silent save the sound of the cannula forcing oxygen into Lexi's small nasal passage. Her slender legs rested over top of Ricky's. The words that the doctor had spoken pulled at their emotions as if they were victims in an unspeakable medieval torture device.

I know it's hard to hear but all of the memories you thought you'd experience with each other, all of the plans you have been making together, most likely won't happen if this is what I think it is.

Ricky's mind replayed the vile words again and again like a worn-out track that he wished he could burn.

Their souls groaned at the disconnect and came crashing back together as the love they had for one another refused the separation, imposed by their impending future.

"I don't know what to say," Lexi said honestly. Her shoulders fell forward in an effort to protect her battered heart from further damage. A single tear slid down her cheek. Ricky let a tear of his own go in direct response to hers. They had celebrated their two-year anniversary only a month ago. The last two years had been filled with experiences and adventures they would carry with them forever. Lexi enrolled in school and began completing her education towards becoming a nurse. Ricky worked as a salesman in many different professions as he tried to find his groove in the adult world. With Lexi's encouragement, Ricky eventually accepted an offer to play basketball for Southern Virginia University. The small town and its inhabitants quickly won their hearts. They met other young couples and enjoyed the adventures that being on their own in a new place offered them. Lexi worked while Ricky fulfilled his dream of playing basketball on a collegiate level. Lexi never missed one of Ricky's games, or an opportunity to tell the refs what she thought about any call involving Ricky. During those games, her lungs seemed to work just fine.

After playing just one year, Ricky began to experience irregular heart palpitations. He was told by his doctors that if he continued to push his body to compete at that level, it could aggravate health conditions later in life. He and Lexi chose to come back home to Utah. They had adopted a puppy and were looking forward to their forever. But, where was their happy ever after? They should be planning how to save for their first home or when to start a family. They should be able to argue overspending too much at the grocery store or whose turn it was to do the dishes. They should have all of the time in the world to grow old together. But Ricky and Lexi did not reside in a "should" world. This was their reality.

"I might have cancer again," Lexi said, trying to hide the tremble in her voice as she stated what they both had already been told. "I don't know if my body is strong enough to handle the treatments a second time. It almost killed me the first time. I almost died. A few times." Her voice trailed off towards the end as the memory of her cancer treatment flashed through her thoughts. She exhaled and pushed through.

"I don't know what things will look like for me in the future. I don't know what my body can or can't handle. I don't know if I am physically strong enough to fight again or if I will die helplessly from the treatment in a blue-walled hospital room surrounded by beeping monitors. Ricky, we both know how ugly cancer is, what the treatment does to a person. We've seen the effects it can have and . . ." She stopped to catch a breath and involuntarily shivered.

Ricky took her hands in his. He rubbed his long thumbs against the backs of her thin hands.

"Lex, I signed up for forever. We signed up for whatever comes. We both knew ahead of time that our lives together weren't going to be easy. I was sicker than you were when we got married. You didn't leave my side. You could have, but you didn't. You stayed with me. I've already had cancer twice and the doctors are surprised you're still alive. We haven't been blessed with physical health. It just wasn't in the cards for us. We knew going in that we aren't like everyone else. But, I don't want anything else. I want you, Lex. I want what we have, whatever that looks like. I've loved you with no hair, with short hair, and now with long hair. I love you forever. We don't know how long we have here, but our love doesn't end here. We have forever."

Lexi leaned forward and gently kissed Ricky. She let her head rest against his as their chemo-beaten hearts synced up once again. Her breath regulated and peace flowed freely from her soul. "Ricky, cancer took away my ability to dance. It took my ability to breathe on my own, and even walk on my own some days. It took memories I wanted to make with Cam, Liv, and Leah. It took my potential to have a family here on earth, and my body's capability to function the way it should. It took my hair, some of my hearing and vision, and even my eyelashes." She looked at him ardently.

He held her gaze and felt her unyielding love for him. Her glistening eyes held his and he could not remember a time that she looked more radiant.

"It took so, so much from me. But I will forever be grateful for this wretched disease," she said. "Because it gave me you."

May 23, 2022

Dear Diary,

Thursday night I had the opportunity to sleep in the front room with Lexi. It wasn't actually sleeping (because she had meds due every two hours), it was more like hanging out on the couch while she slept in Kris's chair. Ricky had opted to sleep downstairs in their room for the past few nights. Lexi was too weak to walk up and down the stairs, and I wanted to stay close in case she needed something throughout the night. As a result, the couch had become my makeshift bed. Her breathing hadn't been great for the last few days—weeks even—but something about the way that she sounded that night had me more worried than usual. As the night progressed, her breathing worsened. It was around 2 a.m. I had just given her the meds that were due. She woke up slightly and I asked if she was comfortable in the chair or if she wanted to come cuddle with me on the couch. She muttered a frail "couch." I helped her stand and wrapped my arms around her waist, as it was evident she would not have the physical strength to walk by herself. To my surprise, she was able to lift both of her arms and place them around me. She purposefully gave me a hug and whispered, "Thank You." Those were the last words I would ever hear my daughter speak in this life.

We slowly made our way to the couch and I helped her get positioned comfortably. I sat right behind her, with the hope that if I kept her body angled in an upright position then she would not have to struggle so hard to breathe. My efforts were in vain. For the next six hours I held her helplessly as I listened to her breathing worsen. I read countless articles on how to help someone near the end of life so that if there was even one thing that I could do to help ease her pain, I would know what it was and how to do it. I recognized how completely and utterly helpless I actually was.

It is said that a person can hear long after they lose the ability to verbally communicate. So, I spoke with her. I sang to her. I cried. Then I did it all again. Her body had lost the ability to respond, but I could feel the strength of her spirit trying to comfort my heart.

Around 8 a.m., Ricky came into the front room. I let him know how she had done through the night and that things were not looking good. He held Lexi while I woke Kris, Liv, and Leah up. I told them what was happening and they each made their way to the front room to be with Lex. The following hours were a mix of family, tears, love, and anguish beyond description. I remember trying to explain the "death rattle" to people so that they would understand that Lexi wasn't feeling any pain. For some reason, I have always felt the need to explain what was happening with Lex. I believed if people could understand just a fraction of what she endured, perhaps they would understand strength, love, and life a bit more clearly.

We spent the entirety of the day taking turns holding Lexi and just being together. Cam was able to call from South Africa and even though Lex could not communicate it, I knew how grateful she was that he had called. Talking to him was a highlight that she looked forward to every week. Lex made me promise months ago that she would not die in the hospital. How grateful I am that we were able to keep that promise. Lex spent the day surrounded by music, a bit of laughter, and so, so much love.

Just after 3 p.m., we learned that although we had continued to turn up the concentrator, Lexi's oxygen levels were steadily declining. Her breathing had become extremely labored. As a family, we opted to remove her cannula. She always hated that thing and we wanted to allow her to be free of it during her transition. Someone turned off the concentrator and I removed the cannula from my daughter's perfect little nose. Ricky had sat beside me and asked if he could hold Lex for a while. I was handing Lexi to Ricky as I heard her take a ragged breath. Lexi opened her beautiful blue eyes wide. She looked directly at Ricky as if trying to communicate something. That was her final breath. "Ricky," I said, "Ricky, I think she's gone." Ricky had been in the process of taking her from my arms, and as he cradled her body, he placed his ear on her heart. "Her heart," he said, "It beat. I heard it beat one more time."

Then her heart, like her breath, stopped. It was 3:33 p.m.

We spent some time as a family holding our beautiful angel. Then, as Ricky continued to hold her, the girls and I opened our front door. We ran into arms that loved Lexi the way we do. The sky let go of the smallest mist of rain drops and I could feel the love and excitement of the long-awaited reunion between Lexi and her angel friends. I knew our girl had completed every last task she had said she would. I knew she ran into the anxiously waiting arms of Christ and then was embraced fully by our Heavenly Father. She laughed with her angels. I felt her laugh and I cried harder.

Lexi's life was lived with purpose. Her death was no exception. Her angel number, 3:33 encourages others to make correct choices in life. In astrology, 333 symbolizes the presence of a guardian angel.

Lex had the opportunity to pass away several times. Her determination and love for those she held close caused her to procrastinate her passing. She suffered in pain so that we would not feel the ache of her loss. Before her passing, she and I had many conversations about life and relationships. She left this world with an understanding of truths that most people do not even recognize exist.

I do not doubt that she will continue to be an active part in each of our lives. She loved us far too much not to be.

Emily

Epilogue

ACCORDING TO THE AMERICAN CANCER SOCIETY, AROUND 700 CHILdren in the United States are diagnosed with neuroblastoma each year. 630 of these children will be diagnosed before the age of five. Rarely is this disease diagnosed in children over ten years old. The older a child is upon diagnosis, the more aggressive the disease is.[1]

Alexis Gould Stafford was diagnosed exactly one month after her fifteenth birthday. Her odds of surviving treatment were low. Her odds of surviving five years and being declared "officially cancer free" were dismal. But, Lexi was more than just a statistic. She was an anomaly.

Not only did Lexi survive treatment, she thrived. Lexi's body endured six rounds of intense chemo, receiving a combination of high dose chemo each time. Four major surgeries, three on an emergency basis, two stem cell transplants, radiation, and antibody therapy. Each of these treatments were considered "standard of care" to treat her type and stage of cancer. After becoming NED (no evidence of disease) Lexi was able to return to high school and even dance again. Although her body would not allow her to compete at the level she had before cancer, her heart refused to quit dancing. She began her senior year with as many credits as a high school sophomore. She worked hard and completed her credits so that she could officially walk and graduate with her class. After graduation, Lexi received her CNA certification. She was very proud to be a CNA. She loved the opportunity to work in a setting that allowed her to care for and

---

1. "Key Statistics About Neuroblastoma," *American Cancer Society,* accessed Jan. 2023, www.cancer.org/cancer/neuroblastoma/about/key-statistics.html.

help others. She looked at it as being one step closer to her dream of becoming a pediatric oncology nurse.

Although Lexi's body had begun to fail just a year after treatment, she did not let that slow her down. Lexi was constantly looking for ways to bring joy and light to all those around her. Lexi held the cancer community particularly close to her heart. She understood firsthand the challenges and suffering that came with a cancer diagnosis and worked to alleviate it in whatever way she could. She organized and participated in fundraisers to help ease the financial burden that accompanied this illness. She remained active in the cancer community and made countless opportunities to spread awareness of childhood cancer. She regularly spent time visiting her cancer friends and felt a special connection to each of them. Over the course of five years, she buried eleven of her close friends. A piece of her heart will forever be buried with each of them.

Lexi and Ricky went on to live their lives to the absolute fullest. They found happiness amongst hospital stays and made magic amidst medications. Lexi loved to travel and never missed an opportunity to go on an adventure. She understood that life was a gift and she gave thanks for that gift every single day. Lexi remained in remission and celebrated being officially cancer free on April 27, 2022. That same day she was placed in hospice for multiple organ failure as a direct result of the lifesaving treatment she had received just a few years before. Her final days were spent among her family and those she loved. Even while on hospice, she attended family sporting events and family parties. She never missed a call with Cam. Lexi joined her eleven angel friends on May 20, 2022 at 3:33 p.m. Her life was lived with purpose. Her death was no exception.

About the Author

EMILY GOULD LOVES TO DISCOVER AS MUCH AS POSSIBLE ABOUT people, cultures, emotions, and the world around her. Emily has been writing for over 20 years. Upon her daughter's cancer diagnosis in September of 2015, writing became less of a hobby and more of a coping mechanism that she used to understand and learn more about herself and the unfamiliar situations her family found themselves in. The more Emily wrote about this foreign world and the lessons learned, the more people listened. Her words have spanned across nations and touched the hearts of people all over the globe. Emily is currently the Utah State Ambassador for The American Childhood Cancer Organization and has recently accepted the position of Leadership Team Chair with the Leukemia Lymphoma Society. She has taken the opportunity to educate those who haven't been afflicted with cancer about the details of the disease in hopes of spreading awareness and love for those who fight for their lives every single day. With her husband Kris by her side, Emily is always up for any adventure that life has to offer. The couple, along with their four children, enjoy camping, hiking, boating, laughing too loud, and just being together.

You can find Emily on Instagram by scanning the QR code.